Into the Jaws of Death

Table of Contents

Into the Jaws of Death

2 Introduction

Into the Jaws of Death

Into the Gates of Hell

Rode the six hundred

That was the way Alfred Lord Tennyson described the Charge of the Light Brigade on 25 Oct 1854 during the Crimean War.

Ninety years later, in the late afternoon, on Tuesday, 24 Oct, 1944, about 600 American sailors set out aboard 39 little wooden motor torpedo boats to take part in what would become the largest naval battle in history. The officers were mostly in their early 20s. The enlisted crewmen were often still only 18 or 19 years old. This is their story.

3 About the Boats

This Chapter focuses on technical details of the boats and tenders. It can be treated as a reference section, or skipped, if you're really only interested in the narrative of the battle.

The Tenders.

MTBs are small, and have a very short range because they don't carry much fuel. The MTB Squadrons that participated in the battle of Surigao Straight had been operating off the New Guinea coast. They had been carried as deck cargo by Navy tankers and cargo ships for the long voyage across the Pacific. Since the boats were of limited endurance, they needed a base ashore or a tender to support them. The boats traveled at an economical speed in order to conserve fuel. The tenders provided them with a mobile home where they could be repaired and replenished as needed. The Squadrons that were involved made the 1300 mile trip from New Guinea to Leyte under their own power. They were accompanied by their tenders, acting as floating gas stations. The tenders were all converted small seaplane tenders of the Barnegat class. Each tender supported one or two squadrons of 10-12 boats each. The tenders had fuel cargo tanks that held about 85000 gallons of gasoline. That fuel could be transferred to the PTs by hoses. The tender slowed to 9 knots and took the PTs in pairs for refueling. One boat was directly astern of the tender. The other was alongside to starboard. Most of the trip was made at 15 knots, an economical speed for the PTs. The route took them first to Kossol Roads at Palau, where they rested for 2 days and made good minor repairs needed as a result of the voyage. The entire group of 45 PTs, 4 tenders, and 2 army aircraft crash boats, set out on 13 Oct, 1944 and arrived at Leyte on 21 Oct. A day later they moved to Liloan Bay from which they departed for their task of reporting the approach of the enemy.

Photo # 19-N-69681   USS Wachapreague on 20 May 1944, port broadside view

The tenders involved were OYSTER BAY (AGP-6), WACHAPREAGUE (AGP-8) and WILLOUGHBY (AGP-9). All of them were converted from Barnegat class small seaplane tenders. A 4th tender, HALF MOON (AVP-26), an unconverted Barnegat class seaplane tender, was also in the convoy. They were all the same size, displacing about 2600 tons when loaded. The tenders were 310'1" long, with a beam of 41' 2" and a draft of 13' 6". They were powered by 4 big diesel engines that produced 6000 HP and could push them through the water at 18 knots. Externally, there were a few small differences. The PT tenders had additional machine shops added aft where the original seaplane tenders had an open deck where an aircraft could be placed for maintenance. The extra space also provided storage room for 48 Mark XIII torpedoes for rearming the PTs. There were special hatches above the storage space where the torpedoes could be lifted out and transferred to a PT. The PT tenders had a single 10 ton boom for handling the torpedoes or moving the PT boats Packard 4M-2500 engines. The tenders had their own crews and, in addition, carried the rear echelon of the MTB squadrons that included medical and dental personnel, repair specialists, cooks and office workers to handle records, personnel files, and correspondence. The tenders handled the following squadrons: OYSTER BAY- MTBRON 33; WILLOUGHBY – MTBRONs 21 and part of 7; WACHAPREAGUE - MTBRONs 12 and 7 (5 boats) The force also supported the 5 boats from MTBRON 36 and an army air corps crash boat, QS-13.

Several boats had damage that was incurred during the trip and were unable to operate on the night of the battle. These included PTs 138, 325, 488, 522 and 525. PT 525 had carried General Douglas Macarthur and other top commanders from their flagship to the beach at Leyte on Oct 23rd. Her skipper was 24 year old

Into the Jaws of Death

Jacksonville, Florida, native, LTJG Alexander W. Wells.
By the end of the war he had been awarded a Silver Star
and a Navy Commendation Medal .On Oct 25th his boat,
along with several other boats, was not ready for action.

The Boats.

The idea of a fast small boat able to avoid detection and
deliver a serious blow with a torpedo was not
something new. It had been around since the first
torpedoes were invented. The earliest torpedoes were
little more than an explosive charge on the end of a
stick. Jab the stick into your enemy and ignite the
charge and he will at least be severely damaged, if not
sunk outright. Such vessels had actually been used in
the American Civil War. The next approach was to tow
the charge toward the target. Release it at a longer
range and let inertia carry it forward to make contact.
This version was used effectively in the Russo-Turkish
wars in 1877. Then along came Alfred Whitehead with
the idea of making the torpedo self-propelled. At the
beginning of the 20th century naval theorists were
devoting a lot of thought to how a small, swift, vessel
could dash (or sneak) in, deliver a potentially
devastating attack, and then retire at high speed to
safety. The result was the development of a type of
vessel called a torpedo boat, and it rapidly grew to

become a destroyer. The name Destroyer was actually a shortened form of Torpedo boat Destroyer which was the name used to describe turn of the century escorts designed to protect larger warships from torpedo attack. The motor torpedo boat was a return to the original idea of a much smaller craft The US Navy ran a competition before the US entry to the war to select the best design for such a craft. There were two big winners, and one other that was selected for production. The Higgins design was used in large numbers in the European theater. It won't be discussed further. Neither will the Huckins design that was employed to defend the Panama Canal. But the Electric Launch Company, usually abbreviated to ELCO, produced a design that became the standard type used by the US Navy in the Pacific. The ELCO design evolved into an 80 foot long version that equipped all the MTB Squadrons that were involved in the Battle of Surigao Strait in 1944.

Hulls built upside down   ptboatforum

Inside the hull.

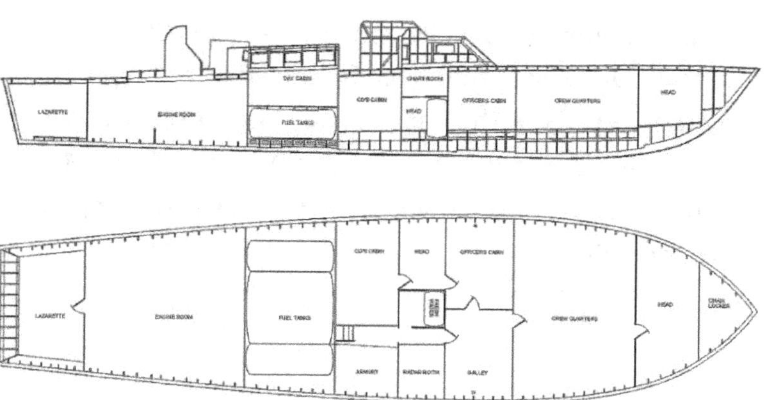

The ELCO 80 foot long motor torpedo boat was built
from wood. It started with the construction of the hull.
The outline of the main deck was laid out and the hull
was built upside down. Framing timbers were attached

to join the main deck with a centerline keel. The bow was sharp at the waterline but flat at the stern. The line where the pointed bow transitioned to the flat stern was called the chine. As the boat went faster, more of the bow rose out of the water and the boat planed on the flatter after surface much like a person skiing or surfing. The frames were covered with a layer of wooden 1x2 inch boards. These then were covered with a layer of canvas impregnated with glue. On top the canvas another layer of mahogany timbers was placed diagonally to give the added strength of not having the grain of the wood of the two layers aligned. Plywood is manufactured in a similar manner, but the PT hulls were not made from plywood. When the hull was complete it was turned over so the rest of the vessel could be built. In fact, most of the upper structure was built separately and attached after the hull was rotated. At this point the description will go from bow to stern inside the hull and then again, from bow to stern on the upper deck.

The space at the forward end was referred to as the chain locker. In order not to waste space, that tiny compartment was utilized to store the sea anchor and anchor chain. Next to the chain locker, as the hull widened, there was the crew's head. On the port side there was a double stainless steel wash basin. A single movable faucet served both sinks. The water flow was controlled by a hand lever and the drain exited from underneath directly into the sea. A counter was built in near the sinks. A toilet was placed on the opposite side of the compartment, facing forward, and there were hand rails behind and to the side to make it a little easier to position one's self on the toilet seat. Another hand rail was on the opposite side, near the sinks. There was even a holder for a roll of toilet paper on the left side. This was a substantial improvement over conditions on the original torpedo boats of half a century earlier. On those boats the crew had to relieve themselves into the sea while standing on the main deck Of course, there were still no showers. The men on PT boats bathed when they were ashore, or on their tender mother ships. Since the hull flared out as it approached the main deck the resultant space near the toilet was used for medicine cabinets on both sides. There was also a mirror on the forward bulkhead. The wooden frames in the overhead were supplied with coat hooks. No one wanted to waste space in such a small vessel.

The next compartment going aft was the crew's quarters. There were bunks for eight men located in pairs, two upper and two lower, on either side. The center of the forward bulkhead had a set of six lockers with the curtain separating the head just alongside. Two more lockers were located on the after bulkhead near the watertight door leading aft. The door could be secured using 6 rotating levers called dogs. When the door was closed and watertight it was referred to as being "dogged down". The center of the compartment had a mahogany topped table attached to tubular supports bolted to the deck. The table had one drawer and drop down leafs on both sides. The corners of the table were rounded, to prevent injury, and the entire edge was raised to prevent items from sliding off in rougher weather. A CO2 fire extinguisher was mounted on the side of one of the wooden main frames. Many boats serving in tropical waters managed to acquire small electric fans and these, too, were attached to the frames .There was space alongside the bunks for additional stowage where the hull flared out.

The next space aft was divided. On the port side was the officer's stateroom. Here, in addition to the two bunks, there was a desk with a top that folded upward, and a book shelf above it on one bulkhead. On the other was a locker/dresser with a mirror above it and the door to the officer's head. Opposite the stateroom was the galley. It was very compact. In the small space it occupied there was a small refrigerator that was even equipped with 4 ice trays. There was also a two burner electric stove, a counter with a porcelain sink (later replaced by one made of aluminum or stainless steel) and fitted with a single lever controlled faucet. Storage space for cups, mess trays, cutlery, and food was provided both above and below the counter. In actual use, the galley usually had a pot of coffee on the stove and was only used to prepare meals when the boats were on patrol, away from their tender. The bins were supposed to hold rations sufficient for as long as four days. The boats were only rarely away from their home base or tender for such a long period. The food stored most often was the standard "C" rations. A C ration carton contained 8 tins. Three of them were standardized meals containing some kind of meat and vegetables and expected to provide one man with one good meal. They were paired with a second tin that included some coffee, crackers, a chocolate dessert, and 'canned heat' to use to warm up the meal. The remaining space included a few sheets of toilet paper, matches, and a can opener, some powder for making a fruit flavored drink, and dried instant coffee powder. The standard cartons were often supplemented in the field with powdered milk, powdered eggs, and even tinned meat from Hormel that would become widely known after the war as SPAM.

There was sometimes no cook assigned to the individual boats and the job of preparing meals was then handled by a crewman with another specialty. PT boat crew members did a lot of cross-training so they could fit in at almost any other position if another man was injured or incapacitated. Cooks served as gunners or loaders when at battle stations.

The door leading aft from the galley passed the radar room, located on the starboard side, and the fresh water tank located on the center line. Aft of the radar room was the armory, a storage space for small arms. There was a shelf with cut outs for storing rifles with an additional wooden strip above it to hold the ends of the barrels. The spacing was originally meant to hold 4 Springfield model 1906 bolt action rifles, but later it was host to Garand M-1 semi-automatic rifles, Thompson sub-machine guns, and M-1 carbines. Above the rifle storage the specifications originally called for a rack to hold 4 cutlasses. Who made that particular rack part of the specifications for a mid-twentieth century warship is not recorded. The armory in later boats was replaced by a wardroom with padded benches on both sides of a fixed mahogany table.

The door leading aft from the stateroom went to the officer's head. The head was located between the stateroom and the captain's cabin. It was similar to the crew's head, but only about half as big. The Captain had a bed with a mattress, and there was another foldable bunk above it. He also was provided with a 5 drawer dresser and a closet, from deck to overhead, with hanging room for uniforms and coats. The space above his dresser was where the boat's glass doored master key rack was placed.

The bulkhead abaft the CO's cabin had no doors. A ladder leading up was located at the end of the passageway to the galley. The bridge and pilot house were above the officer's quarters. Abaft the bulkhead just mentioned were the three 3000 gallon fuel tanks for the engines. Each engine could use up to 200 gallons per hour at high speed. That translates to an endurance of only 15 hours. The boats didn't operate at full speed all the time, so their endurance was normally much longer. Above those fuel tanks was what was called the day room. It will be covered as part of the main deck.

This takes us to the engine room. It housed 3 salt water cooled Packard 4M-1600 Marine gasoline engines. Each engine drove one of the three aluminum-manganese-bronze right hand turning propellers. The propellers were three bladed and about 30 inches in diameter. With all 3 engines at full power an ELCO boat could travel at more than 40 knots. The boat's electric generators were also located in this space. The center engine was a bit forward of the ones on either side. The generators were located outboard, next to the hull. Each engine had a set of mufflers on the exhaust line that could be disconnected when the boat needed maximum power and avoiding detection was not a problem. The mufflers were actually positioned outboard of the fantail aft. Each of the engines also had a set of meters and controls mounted on it and a matching set was located inside the pilot house. The only voice tube on the boat connected the engine room to the bridge. Although the boat could travel at about 40 knots, it was not something that was normally done. Tactically, a PT boat was expected to sneak up, undetected, to torpedo launching range. Once the torpedoes had been launched it was time to escape. Even then, unless actually detected by the enemy, the boat would withdraw at slow speed until the torpedo had reached their target. Then it was time to open the throttles and run as fast as possible. At high speeds the boat threw up a high 'rooster-tail' wake that was easy to see. If the wake was spotted before the torpedoes struck the target would have time to maneuver to evade.

The last compartment, right aft of the engine room, was called the lazarette. It contained the steering motors for the rudders and a work bench with a selection of tools.

It was also used for storage and the 2 spare propellers were kept there.

On the main deck.

The first thing encountered on the bow is the jack staff, and immediately behind it, the anchor. The entire main deck has a raised "toe rail" placed just far enough from the edge of the deck to alert a man that he is about to step off into the sea. Also near the bow is one of the many cleats used to tie up the boat to another vessel or to the shore. Weapons will be covered later. The next obvious item is one of the deadlights that admit light into internal compartments, but are enclosed, and cannot be opened. This first one lets light into the chain locker and the next 4 illuminate the crew's compartment during the day. There are hatches on the main deck leading to both of these spaces. The next item is the cockpit or pilot house. It is enclosed, and has deadlight windows both forward and on either side. Inside the cockpit is the chart room, a table for navigation placed atop a set of drawers containing navigational charts. Alongside the chartroom are the operator's positions for the radio and radar. The 20 foot long whip antenna for the radio is outside on the port side. Inside, the Collins model CMX 46159, also known as a TCS-12, is on a table with the operator's chair alongside it. The radio works in the VHF band from 1.5 to 12MHz. There is a portable Aldis lamp used for visual signaling stored inside the pilot house; and a set of semaphore flags under the counter. A flag bag, with all the necessary signal flags, and a small searchlight are located on the side of the bridge, just behind the pilot house. The international port and starboard navigational lights, not used in the war area, are located on the sides of the pilot house.

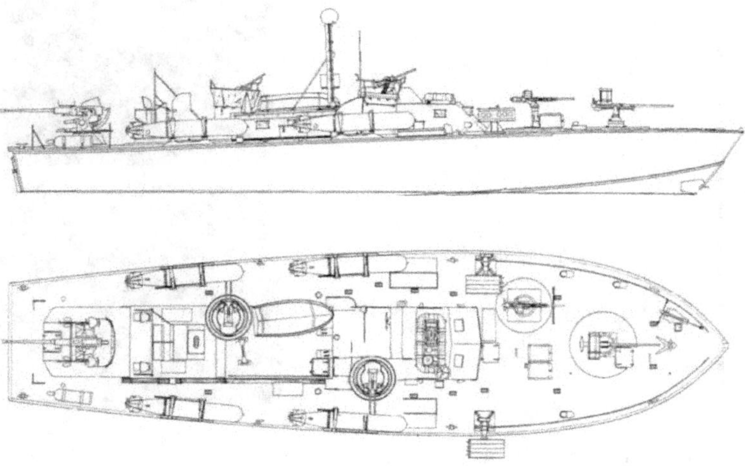

The diagram above shows rocket launchers with the one on the port side in stowed position and the one to starboard ready for firing.

Into the Jaws of Death

The simple torpedo sight is in the center of bridge, where it can be used to aim torpedoes from either side. Directly behind the captain is the starboard twin 0.50 caliber mount. The matching port side mount is further aft, behind the day room. The short mast, topped by the antenna for the SO-1 radar, is located behind the bridge, on the forward edge of the day room, just behind the ladder leading down to the inner hull.

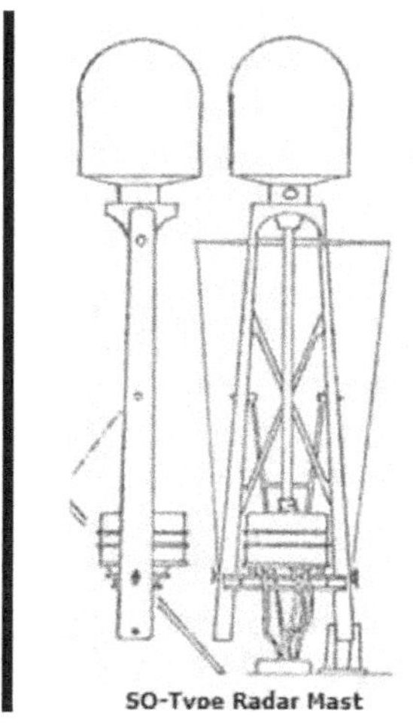

Left – Type SO Radar Mast

Right TBS (Top) and TCS-12(Bottom) radios

By 1944 the electronic IFF (Identification Friend or Foe) system was already in use. It was based on a pulsed radar signal that was sent from one ship that engendered an automatic pulsed reply from another. PTs were too small to carry the interrogation system, but they were equipped with the automatic response equipment in order to provide information that could help avoid incidents of shooting at a friendly vessel. IFF transponders were added to PTs as a field modification when enough equipment became available.

 The day room had another pair of foldable berths. Actually, they were roll-up berths, but in practice they were most often left unrolled, and crew members napped there. The storage bins contained medical supplies and the hatch/door leading out was designed to be large enough to allow the passage of a stretcher. The hatch to the engine room and the large air vent to the engine room were located behind the day room.

The 40mm Bofors cannon took up the remaining space aft. The lazarette had the mufflers mounted outboard of the after bulkhead. Just at the edge of the deck aft was where most boats carried their smoke generator. The smoke generator was a fancy name for a compressed gas bottle made of steel and containing about 35 gallons of titanium tetrachloride gas. When the gas came in contact with humid air it formed a dense cloud of white smoke. The gas in the cylinder was sometimes referred to as tickle gas, based on the chemical formula TiCl4. But this gas was not ticklish. It was actually quite corrosive and could even be toxic. One of the byproducts of the gas was hydrochloric acid. When used to make a smoke screen, it was released from the pressurized cylinder and it formed an immediate screen that could visually hide the movements of the boat from an enemy that was in pursuit. Three turns of the valve wheel on the steel container would open it completely. Fewer turns could be made to control the rate of release.

Weapons:

PTs carried more ordnance per ton of displacement than any other warship.
The 80 foot Elco design was built in several sequences. Each group had a slightly different original weapons fit. But once overseas, the armament underwent changes. The heavy torpedo tubes of the early PT boats were all replaced by 1944 with a simple, side launching rack, with a Mark XIII aerial torpedo nested in it. One example was PT-127. That boat was overhauled in February, 1944. Her older torpedo tubes were replaced with the new racks and she had a 40mm gun added aft. At the end of her overhaul she had added a lot of new weapons. This prompted QM3c Thomas Edward Tenner

to comment "When the forty was installed we thought we were a battleship. That was the way it was."1

Left to Right: 40mm, 20mm, and 37mm guns

Torpedoes:

Early PT boats carried 2 to 4 of the standard Mark VIII surface ship torpedoes housed in torpedo tubes that could be trained a few degree outboard. By late 1944 the heavy tubes had all been removed and replaced by a much lighter roll-off side launching rack. The heavy Mark VIII torpedoes were replaced by the Mark XIII that had been originally designed to be carried by aircraft. A cable held the torpedo in place on the rack. When launching, the torpedoman pulled a lever that released that cable. As the torpedo rolled off into the water a smaller line was pulled out that activated the torpedo motor.

---

[1] Voices p67

PT-490 torpedo launch drill   Navsource 120549005

40mm:

The largest gun carried by the PTs was a crew served 40mm, Bofors design, automatic cannon. The Bofors wasn't included in the as-built boats in any of PTs that were at Surigao. All of them had it added as an in the field modification. The pointer and trainer had bicycle style seats on either side of the gun mount. Foot pedals controlled the electric motors that moved the mount and/or gun from side to side and up and down. The other 2 members of the gun crew were loaders. They stood near the mount and supplied a steady stream of ammunition for the gun. The 40mm shells came in 4 round clips that the loaders dropped into the loading guide rails on the top of the gun. Spare ready ammunition was located in bins forward of the mount. Ultimately, a framework of pipes was positioned to keep the barrel of the gun from ever being pointed at any part of the boat. The Surigao boats did not have this installed. In the original ELCO designs the location of the 40mm had been taken by a single 20mm cannon.

37mm:

The forward gun mount of the boats was a 37mm cannon. Here, too, the original equipment was either no gun forward, or a 20mm cannon. The 37mm was operated by one man. Another was assigned to keep the curved upper magazine supplied with shells. The first installations were adapted from the gun designed for use in the P-39 fighter aircraft. Later models were manufactured specifically for PTs by the Oldsmobile Auto Company in Michigan..

20mm:

37mm bow gun on PT-190

The 20mm Oerlikon cannon that originally was carried aft was relocated to the forward deck, portside, just ahead of the cockpit. The 20mm used portable magazines containing 30 rounds. Several spare magazines were stored in a locker in front of the pilot house. In the field modifications added more 20mm guns, sometimes forward, and sometimes in place of the twin 0.50 machine guns. A few boats carried a mount that combined the 20mm with a single 0.50 caliber machine gun. It was known as the Acey-Deucy mount.

0.50 caliber:

The standard PT boat machinegun battery was two twin gun mounts in little gun tubs on the two sides of the bridge. The starboard mount was just behind the captain's chair and the port side mount was located at the after end of the day room. Ammunition came in boxes of 250 linked rounds. Spare boxes were on the inside of the gun tub. As with the 40mm mount, a pipe frame on each of the tubs was later added to keep the gunners from shooting at parts of their own boat.

Depth Charges:

PT boats were not designed to fight submarines. They had no Sonar gear. But depth charges could be carried in place of torpedoes. Dropping a depth charge over the side might also be used to create a large splash that would confuse enemy gunners. The charges could be used against a submarine that had just submerged, or at very close range, to help sink an enemy barge.

Rockets:

In late 1944 the Navy came up with a number of designs for firing 4.5" or 5" spin stabilized rockets, primarily at shore targets. Some PTs had launchers bolted to the deck on either side, slightly forward of the pilot house. The launchers carried 8 rockets each, and would be folded outboard for firing. Boats fitted with these launchers usually also carried 8 extra rockets per launcher for reloads.

60mm Mortar

PT-132 test firing a mortar

PT boats often found themselves in action at very close quarters. Some boats got their hands on army 60mm or 81mm mortars and attached them to the deck so that they would have some additional fire power capable of delivering destruction to targets where the standard , line of sight, weapons could not always be employed. But in most cases, the mortars were used for firing illumination rounds at night.

Armory weapons (rifle, SMG, pistols, carbines):

In action against enemy barges carrying troops and supplies individual crew members might employ small caliber weapons from the armory, or individual side arms for the officers. Weapons also came in handy for guarding prisoners on the rare occasions when Japanese surrendered.

Communication plans:

The only electronics carried by the PTs were an SO-1 radar and TCS radios. During the battle for Leyte the PTs used the circuits assigned them. These were voice common on 3115 KHz and 142.74 MHz VHF.

Small craft visual and radio recognition signals changed at 0001Z every day. Leyte was in zone I, some 9 hours earlier than Greenwich. That meant changes took place about 0900 local time. On 24 Oct. Day recognition for small craft was RDU and at night it was GUM. Most boats had a little chalk board on the bridge where the current small craft challenge and response were written.

The standard MTB voice call sign for individual PTs was Webfoot (plus a number).

Often, in order to keep enemy listeners from intercepting communications, messages were sent by using semaphore or flashing light, Sometimes printed messages were delivered by high line, as in the following illustration.

PT-523 receiving a hi-line message   Navsource 120552302

Camouflage and markings:

This can be seen on the photographs of individual boats. But as a general rule the following standards were followed:

Camouflage was uniform within each squadron. But the squadrons each carried different colors or patterns.

MTBRON 7 boats were painted overall green with red numbers and white shadowing

MTBRON 12 boats wore pattern Measure 31/5P.

MTBRON 21 boats were painted using pattern Measure 31/20L.

MTBRON 33 Pts sported overall green paint with an aircraft style white star in a blue circle on the cockpit (and sometimes also aft atop the day room). They also had a shadow on their red boat numerals.

MTBRON 36 boats were green overall.

In addition, the boats and squadrons had their own version of heraldry. Boat nicknames were often painted on the cockpit, usually on the front. Squadron emblems, when displayed, were on the side of the pilot house, near the running lights. Boats that had success in combat displayed a score card on the side of the cockpit with hash marks indicating how many of what kind of Japanese craft they had destroyed. The boat number was also painted there, and on many boats that was where the nickname appeared.

The following are official designated camouflage designs for ELCO MTBs. The measure number set the colors to be used. For example, design 7P could be applied in Measure 31, 32, or 33. Measure 31 used 5 Ocean Green and Dull Black on the sides and 20 Green on the Deck. MTB Green, a mixture of 4 parts Ocean Green and 1 part Navy Green, could be used in place of 5- Ocean Green.

Measure 32 called for 5-Ocean Green in place of Black, and 5 Pale Green in place of Ocean Green. Here, too, 5 Light Gray might be used instead on Pale Green. On the horizontal surfaces, such as the decks, a combination of 20 Green and 5 Ocean Green could be applied.

These were guidelines set by the Camouflage design teams at the Bureau in Washington. In the field, the crews often mixed their own colors and, earlier in the war, even made up their own designs. Design 7P was not used on boats at Surigao.

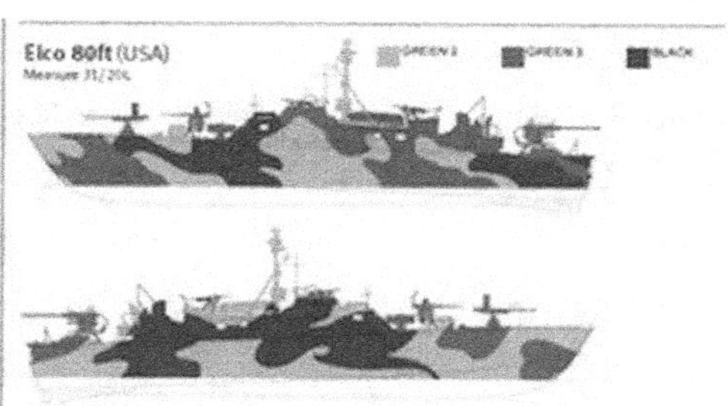

Measure 31 design 20L

Into the Jaws of Death

Measure 31 design 5P

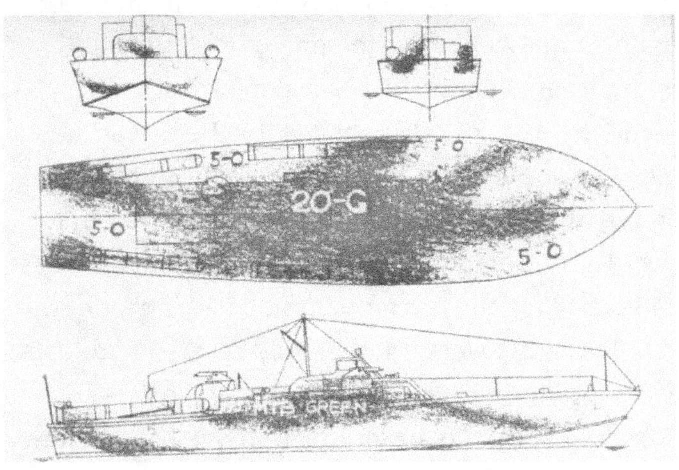

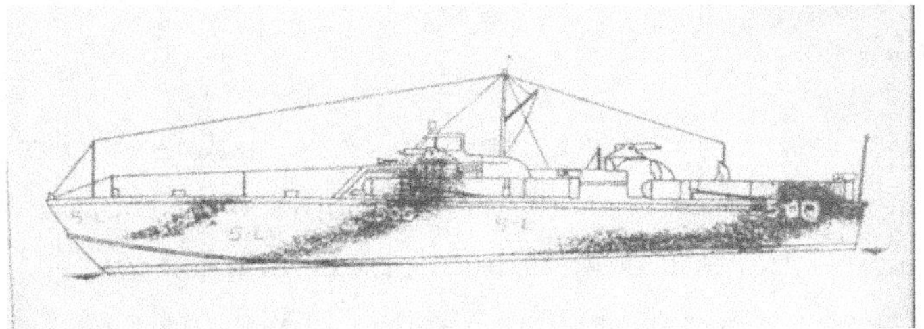

ELCO MTB Measure 31 design 7P

4 About the Crews

The Japanese attack on Pearl Harbor was not intended to occur before war was declared, but a variety of mishaps caused it happen before the formal declaration was made. In America the event was uniformly taken to be a cowardly attack made outside the accepted rules of war. This resulted in a massive wave of patriotic volunteering for military service. Young men left school to sign up. Some waited for the end of the current semester, others did not. The wave of patriotic involvement was partly responsible for their later receiving the appellation as 'The Greatest Generation'. The United States already had a registration system for drafting eligible personnel in place. The various services also had plans in place for mobilizing and training new recruits. Reservists were immediately called up. Industry quickly shifted to producing war material. Both regular recruiters and special teams were employed to ask new recruits to volunteer for special jobs. PT boat duty was one of them.

PT boat crews were teams. There were usually 2 officers assigned to each boat. They were supported by about 14 enlisted men. All were volunteers. PT combat was expected to occur in close proximity to the enemy. Torpedoes had to be launched at close range in order to be effective. The guns carried were only effective at short range. The conditions on board could never be called luxurious. But the PT sailors knew this when they signed on. PT sailors wore a small cloth badge on their lower right sleeve with the letters 'P T' inside a circle to indicate their special status. Unlike aviation or submarine duty, PT duty did not get you extra hazardous duty pay. During World War II, and until well after the war (1949), Navy uniforms differed from what we are used to seeing today. Navy petty officers in deck or seaman categories (e.g., boatswains mate, signalman, gunner's mate, quartermaster, and torpedo man's mate) wore their insignia of rank only on the right sleeve of the their uniforms and were referred to as right arm rates. Petty officers in artificer and engine room categories (e.g., radioman, machinist mate, and electrician) wore insignia on the left sleeve and were referred to as left arm rates. Prior to reaching petty officer status right arm rates were called seaman 1st class and left arm rates fireman 1st class.

To start with, they were all volunteers. And they were all young. Fighting wars is an occupation usually reserved for young men. Officers usually volunteered for PT duty while they were still receiving their basic military education. The Navy Bureau of personnel examined the files of the volunteers. Actual selection often involved careful screening for ambitious, action oriented, competitive individuals. Participating in team sports was one indicator that helped in getting chosen for PT duty.

Almost everyone in the PT squadrons was new to the navy. The officers were invariably shown with USNR after their name. That stood for U S Naval Reserve. Other ship types often had a scattered number of Annapolis graduates, the PT squadrons did not. For many, knowledge of naval history, customs, and traditions, was limited to a few short lectures during their initial training. But that could also be said about much of the specific training they received before going off to the war zone. Here is a typical story of how an officer joined the PT fraternity.

Richard William Brown was a 1941 Villanova graduate in economics when Japan attacked Pearl Harbor. He joined the navy and was sent to an indoctrination course at Dartmouth before receiving his commission as an Ensign, USNR on June 12th, 1942. Brown, a New Yorker, volunteered for MTB duty. He was always known as Bill. Despite his glasses and short stature (he was 5'7" tall) he had played football as a backup quarterback in college. He stated "PTs were a really tricky outfit to get into. Before deciding to go to Villanova I'd gotten an appointment to Annapolis; and as a teenager I'd also been to sea during the summer on vessels of the Red D steamship line. So I thought these experiences helped get me into PTs. Then I found I didn't make as big a splash as I thought with the people who selected me. Actually it was my mother who got me in. And that surprised me because my father was killed in World War I, and I figured she wouldn't want me in any dangerous type of program. But she worked for an admiral in the Third Naval District and she got him to pull some strings, although I didn't find out until later"2

Brown, himself, said that his friend, Harley Andrew Thronson, was the person who influenced his own decision to ask for PTs. Bill was selected to be the skipper of PT-493 which was them under construction at the ELCO factory. Thronson got command of PT-491. Another officer, Joseph Beckman, was commanding officer of PT-497 in the same squadron. When Bill Brown remarried in 1956, after his first wife had died 2 years earlier, Joe Beckman was his best man.

Another member of this close knit band of brother officers was Californian Terry Macdonald Chambers. He would later serve as second officer under both Brown

---

2 Voices p33-34

and Thronson. He was in his junior year at Pomona College when the US entered the war.

"I grew up in Southern California, pretty close to the ocean and spent summers on Catalina Island teaching swimming, lifesaving, and sailing at a Boy Scout Camp. Unlike some people from the East Coast who'd grown up with their Daddy's yacht, I'd grown up a product of the Depression. My family's orange ranch went flat ass broke" Terry related.3

Chambers dropped out of college and made for the nearest navy recruiting office. His experience with small boats got him rated as a coxswain and he was assigned to lead an armed guard detachment on a civilian liberty ship in the Pacific. A year later, in the summer of 1943, he was ordered to Northwestern University for a naval officer's indoctrination course. Terry talked about that experience.

"Off duty I hung out at the Chicago Yacht Club, caging drinks and crewing on some of the members' boats. Near the end of training, a guy named Murray Preston came out from the PT school in Melville, Rhode Island, looking for PT volunteers. Ultimately I got assigned in Melville and ended up in RON 33, which Murray

---

[33] Voices p 34

commanded. Melville was a great place to be, at least until it got cold."4

Harley Thronson, mentioned above, was another Preston acquisition. Six foot tall Thronson came from Chippewa Falls, Wisconsin. But winter at Melville was different from winter in the mid-west. "I was used to the cold, just not this soaking wet kind of cold." He said.5

Enlisted men went to boot camp, followed for many by a technical school and then MTB training. Specialty schools were needed for several occupations. Each PT normally needed at least one each of the following; Quartermaster (QM) Signalman (SM), Radioman (RM), Gunners Mate (GM), Torpedo man's mate (TM), and Motor Machinists Mate (MoMM). Others reported for duty as seamen (S1c) and learned on the job. As already noted all were volunteers and also went to MTB School at Melville.

Thomas Edward Tenner joined the navy on January 12th, 1943. In a post-war interview with the Lubbock Avalanche Journal he stated "It was an easy thing to go

---

4 ibid
5 Ibid,

into the war. They didn't have a draft. They had more volunteers than they could handle".

"Some people were middle class, some people were poor. We were about three grades lower than poor."

"When I went into the service, most military people moaned about food, and moaned about hard sleeping conditions. But I never had it so good." Tenner remembered.6
He went to a navy school for quartermasters after basic training. He volunteered for PTs in August, 1943, but he didn't get to the MTB School until October. His recollection of Rhode Island in the winter was not good.

"I spent October, November and December in Melville training on boats in the North Atlantic. It was freezing and damn rough. So my first impression of the PT boat was I hated it.7" He said.

Tenner continued, "When it came time for assignment, about half of the guys were scheduled to go right away as replacements to the South Pacific while the other half waited in Melville to pick up new squadrons. I was selected to stay and pick up a new squadron, which

---

[6] Lubbock Avalanche Journal
[7] Ibid

meant I'd have to be in Melville for the rest of the winter and maybe in the North Atlantic afterwards – something I didn't want. And I was restless. I'd been in the navy for a year and hadn't even been shot at."

"It just so happened I was talking with another quartermaster who was scheduled to go to the Pacific. He was married and hoped to spend more time in the States near his wife. I was just the opposite. I wanted to get out of there. So we asked about switching places, and they let us do it. So I was off by train to California." He said.[8]

Tom Tenner said "I landed in New Guinea at the end of January, 1944 and was assigned to PT-127".

According to the muster rolls, he joined MTBRON7 on February 6th, 1944.[9] The weather there at that time of the year was marked by high humidity, torrential rains and an average temperature of close to 26 degrees C (80 degrees F). That was quite a difference from Rhode Island.

Neither doctor dentist, hospital corps man (PhM) nor administrative trades like yeomen (YN) or personnel men (PN) were in the boat crews. Normally, only one

---

[8] Voices p35
[9] MTBRON 7 muster rolls.

ship's cook (SC) and no bakers (BK) were assigned either. They served with the squadron command group. Carpenters (CM), storekeepers (SK), shipfitters (SF), electricians (EM), and metalsmiths (MS) did not appear in the MTB crews at all. These jobs existed at the squadron level and the men who were trained in these specialties served in the tenders, but not in the boats except occasionally as extra 'guests' along for the ride or experience.

Training at Melville, RI, the site of the MTB training school culminated with assignment to new boats and squadrons (or to replacement pool for units already deployed). New boats were typically organized in squadrons of 10 to 12 boats. The boats were not regarded as commissioned ships. The Navy administered the MTB Squadrons in a manner similar to that used for aircraft squadrons. Squadron headquarters handled administration and major maintenance problems. Squadron manning allowances included administrative personnel like YN, SK, PhM, StM, PN and BK. They normally were not part of boat crews. These men were based on the tenders that acted as mother ships to the boats. They provided medical and dental services, repair shops, hot food, and resupply of fuel and munitions. The remainder of the personnel was assigned to specific boats as crew members.

Replacements were sent out to join existing squadrons after completing MTB School in RI. For those destined for the South Pacific, this usually meant reporting to San Francisco and catching a ride in a ship heading west. In March, 1944 the troopship GENERAL B L HOWZE (AP-134) carried almost 4999 passengers. Among them were a dozen officers bound for service with MTBRONSSEVENTHFLT. In July USS GANYMEDE (AK-104) embarked several officers going to the same place. One of them was a doctor.

Another point that needs to be made here is that the crews were all white. The US military was still segregated. The only jobs available for blacks in the navy were in food service and as stevedores. Of course, after Pearl Harbor no one was willing to even think about taking Asians into the ranks. For some Asian actors in Hollywood this became an opportunity. Asian actors were in demand to play the 'bad guy' parts in films. Chinese Richard Loo (actually born in Hawaii) and Korean Philip Ahn built their careers from this. Ahn, who was actually born in California, thought of it as his patriotic duty. He actually enlisted in the Army, but was discharged after suffering an ankle injury. His younger brother joined the Navy after high school. His sister, Susan Ahn, became the first Korean-American woman in the US Navy. She went to officer indoctrination at Smith College and was assigned as an aerial gunnery instructor. She finished the war as a full Lieutenant.

5 About the War

Japan attacked the US at Pearl Harbor with the expectation that there would be a relatively short war that would be concluded by a Japanese victory. That victory would be either a decisive military triumph or an acceptance of Japanese War aims by her adversaries. As far as I know, this expectation was never stated explicitly. All of Japan's military leaders knew how every war that Japan had been in in the past half century had ended in such a way. In 1894 Japan had made demands on the Chinese. The Chinese Empire refused to accept the Japanese dictated terms. The resulting war was marked by the Japanese Navy soundly defeating the Chinese fleet at the battle of the Yalu, and laying siege to the remnants of the Chinese fleet in Wei-Hai-Wei. Japanese armies occupied Korea. A later Chinese 'popular' rebellion against foreigners present in Japan that became known as the Boxer Rebellion simply made the weakness of the Chinese Empire even more apparent. Other European powers began to step in and squeeze the Japanese out of their expected winnings. This led to yet another war, the third in ten years. This time 'little' Japan took on the Russians. The Russian fleet of 1904 was the second largest in the world. Only Britain's Royal Navy was larger. Undeterred, the Japanese struck at the Russian Pacific Squadron drove them into a blockade at Port Arthur (now called Liaoyang). The Japanese army advanced through Korea, routed the Russian armies that opposed them, and captured Port Arthur. A Second (combined with a third) Russian Pacific Squadron made an epic voyage from the Baltic all the way to the Far East, only to be nearly annihilated by the Japanese fleet at Tsushima. This war, too, ended with a victorious Japan reaping the benefits won by her armed forces. It should also be noted that Japanese society and culture are filled with examples of self-sacrifice for the good of the emperor. The warrior's code, Bushido, exemplifies this dedication. Japanese soldiers and sailors who lived during this era would rather die than surrender.

Another decade passes and Europe is drawn into the crucible of the First World War. Japan waits a bit, and then sides with the allied powers. Japanese forces only participate to the extent needed to reap the benefits. Japan gains almost all of what had been Imperial Germany's Asian colonies. The world, in reaction to the horror of the conflict, forms the League of Nations and engages on the first great effort to limit armaments. Warships constitute the most obvious target for arms limitation because they are so big, and so expensive. Japan seeks parity with Great Britain in this field, but is not completely successful. The London and Washington warship limitations agreements grant Japan a position ahead of the lesser naval powers of Europe, France and Italy, but still well behind the Royal Navy and the United States. It's an achievement, but not as big as what they wanted.

In China, the Empress is deposed and a Republic is formed. Local Chinese warlords are not fully controlled by the new central government. Sensing Chinese weakness, Japan begins to expand into territory that was formerly part of the Chinese Empire. A relative of the former Chinese ruling dynasty is given control over Manchuria, The Japanese control him, and his realm is given the Japanese name Manchukuo. The Japanese military, however, has an even bigger appetite. A border incident is 'manufactured' so that new, greater, demands can be made on China. This time, there is no other foreign intervention, and the Chinese simply refuse to surrender. Between 1931 and 1940 Japan physically occupies most of China's commercial ports and significant portions of the interior. Japanese armies are better equipped and better trained than their opponents. The Chinese lose battle after battle, but just retreat after each engagement. Continuing to pursue the war is expensive. It's not only money that is a problem, Japan needs fuel, steel, and munitions. America threatens to embargo trade with Japan if the war isn't ended. Scrap iron and oil no longer flow from America to Japan. The stage is now set for a wider Pacific War.

When Japan invaded China the USA remained neutral. When Germany began swallowing up her neighbors the USA remained outside the conflict. There was a strong anti-war feeling in America. President Roosevelt recognized that Germany was a major danger and worked to support England, but kept the US out of active participation. The country invested in making preparations for defense. These included preparations for acquiring high speed, short range, motor torpedo boats. Since the US Navy had no such vessels, a design competition was staged to see what American ship and boat builders could offer. This resulted in the formation of motor torpedo boat squadron and a special training base in Rhode Island.

The first squadrons were only put into service in 1941. MTBRON One was formed from the experimental boats and MTBRON Two from the first production runs. Before the Japanese attack on Pearl Harbor there were 29 boats in service. They were assigned to 3 squadrons. MTBRON 3 was scheduled to reinforce the Asiatic Fleet in the Philippines. Six of the squadron's boats were already there when the war began. MTBRON One had been re-equipped with standard boats and was to be assigned to Hawaii. Six of her boats were in Pearl Harbor on December 7th, 1941 and were officially the first to shoot at the attacking Japanese aircraft. MTBRON Two was in Panama

Japanese forces strike at the naval forces of the United States in Hawaii, Guam, and the Philippines. The French, having already been defeated by Nazi Germany, offer no resistance to Japanese occupation of Indo-China. England is struggling against Germany and Italy and can spare little to defend he Asian provinces. Japanese armies overrun Malaysia and capture Singapore. A hastily assembled combined American British Dutch and Australian force cannot stem the Japanese advance that now draws the Dutch East Indies into its' net. But the expected bid for a negotiated peace and compliance with Japanese demands never happens.

The United States needed heroes during the first part of the war. Army Air Corps Captain Colin Kelly, who was killed attacking invading Japanese forces in December 1941, became one of the first. Navy LT John Bulkeley was in command of the PT boats in the Philippines. He managed to take General Macarthur and a handful of other VIPs from Luzon to Mindanao from where they were flown to Australia. The exploit earned him the

Medal of Honor. He was used as a speaker for War Bonds tours before returning to command another PT squadron. MTBRON3 lost all of the boats that were in the Philippines. A New MTBRON3 was created in its' place.

Some New MTBRONs were sent to the South Pacific where they made a reputation for themselves by interrupting Japanese supply lines and sinking enemy small craft and barges throughout the Solomon Islands and New Guinea campaigns. Another squadron was sent to the Aleutians, It was even colder there than at the training base in Rhode Island.

Wherever the MTBRONs were assigned they remained dependent upon having either a tender or a shore base for support. The Navy Construction Battalions (Seabees) came to the locations where bases were needed and built them. The requirements for a PT base were fairly simple; Some structures (usually Quonset huts) for sleeping quarters, galleys and mess halls for food, storage facilities for fuel and ammunition, headquarters and administration structures, piers for the boats, and some support buildings like a post office, a chapel, sanitary facilities (including showers), and often, an outdoor movie theater. When compared to living aboard, such minimal bases were extremely comfortable.

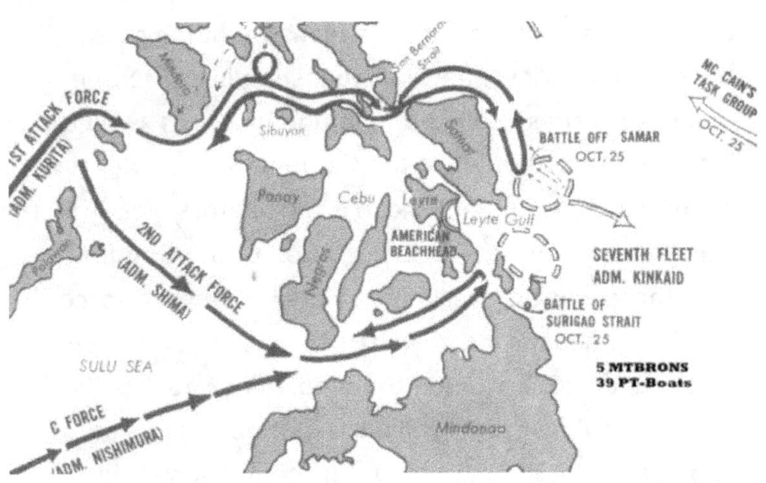

Map of the Naval Battles around Leyte Gulf

6 The Japanese Plan

By late 1944 it was clear that Japan was losing the war. The High Command of the Navy, however, was still prepared to make another attempt at winning a massive, decisive, victory. American submarines were destroying Japanese shipping at a rate that would soon bring Japan to her knees. Neither fuel, nor raw materials, nor foodstuffs were getting through in sufficient amounts. Japanese carrier air groups had lost too many pilots, and the training pipeline was unable to provide enough new ones to make up the losses. The once vaunted naval air arm was truly a paper dragon. Fuel was in such short supply that the combined fleet was now basing almost all of the major warships at southern locations, nearer to fuel supplies. The one item the Japanese still had in abundance was a will to fight. The commander of the Combined Fleet, Admiral Soemu Toyoda, told American interrogators after the war. "Since without the participation of our Combined Fleet there was no possibility of the land-based forces in the Philippines having any chance against your forces at all, it was decided to send the whole fleet, taking the gamble. If things went well we might obtain unexpectedly good results; but if the worst should happen, there was a chance that we would lose the entire fleet; but I felt that the chance had to be taken…Should we lose in the Philippines operations, even though the fleet should be left, the shipping lane to the south would be completely cut off so that the fleet, if it should come back to Japanese waters, could not obtain its fuel supply. If it should remain in southern waters, it could not receive supplies of ammunition and arms. There would be no sense of saving the fleet at the expense of the loss of the Philippines."1011

The resultant overall plan was nearly identical for all the alternate scenarios based on where the Americans would strike next. The US chose to land in the Philippines. Preliminary landings on some small islands by US Army Rangers on October 17th triggered the Japanese fleet response. It came in several, coordinated moves. The main hope was for the battleships and cruisers to fight their way through from the south to destroy the American shipping supporting the invasion force. The carrier force that was trying to rebuild in the Inland Sea would sortie to the south as a diversion to help the battleships get through. Vice-Admiral Jisaburo Ozawa commanded them and they were referred to as the Northern Force. The Center Force was split into 2 groups. The larger body, referred to as Force "A", under

---

[10] USSBS (Pacific) 1945 p317

Vice-Admiral Takeo Kurita, would go around Luzon and approach Leyte from the West. A smaller group, Force "C", under Vice-Admiral Shoji Nishimura, was to come to Leyte from the south via Surigao Straight. An additional unit from the Southwest Area Fleet was sent as a follow up to Force "C". It was commanded by Vice Admiral Kiyohide Shima, and might have been sent separately because Shima was senior to Nishimura, but his ships were not part of what the Japanese called the Mobile Fleet. This conjecture is really not important. What matters is that all the Japanese groups were all intended to converge on Leyte Gulf at the same time.

American intelligence was able to follow what was happening on the Japanese side. Long range reconnaissance by air and submarine patrols kept tabs on the approaching enemy. The main American striking force, The Third Fleet under Admiral William Halsey, was located to the North East and prepared to deal with both the Northern and Center Japanese forces. Seventh Fleet, responsible for the invasion, took steps to protect the gulfs southern approaches. The battleships and cruisers that had been bombarding the beaches were disposed to cover the north end of Surigao Straight. What was still missing was precise data about where the Japanese were located.

On the Japanese side there was the serious problem of providing fuel for the ships. Heavy losses of tankers carrying oil to the home islands had resulted in the necessity of basing most of the combined fleet surface combat ships away from the home islands and closer to fuel supplies in Borneo and the former Dutch East indies. Aircraft carriers remained in Japan because they needed to be nearer to facilities that could provide new aircraft and pilots. Even then, the severe shortage of trained aviators meant that the Japanese capability to engage in carrier air combat was very limited. When these factors were taken into account it meant the only real hope of winning a major naval battle against the Americans rested with the old dream of a successful fleet surface action.

Admiral Toyoda knew the Americans were likely to try to invade and recapture the Philippines. His battle plan was based on destroying the invasion force and then engaging the Americans in a surface fleet action. The US Navy had more aircraft carriers and planes. One salient feature of the Japanese plan was to use their own carrier force that was highly inferior in both numbers of ships and planes and the level of training of pilots, as a diversionary bait to draw off the American carriers while the main surface force penetrated into the area of the landing beaches to destroy the ships that would be supplying the troops ashore. Instead of concentrating his fleet before attacking, the Japanese admiral arranged a coordinated attack by several separate forces that were all intended to meet at the same time off the American invasion beaches. The surface forces would travel in 3 separate groups. The main fleet under VADM Kurita would move from Lingga Roads, near Singapore, via Palawan Passage and the Sibuyan Sea to reach the beaches from the North. The second force, with 2 battleships, commanded by VADM Nishimura, would attack from the South via Surigao Strait. A third force under VADM Shima would follow a similar route and rendezvous off the beaches at Leyte.

The entire Japanese Fleet was still inferior to the American forces in numbers. American radar was better than that of their opponents. American aircraft were better than the planes the Japanese could put in the air, and American aviators were much better trained. But the biggest US advantage came from their intelligence branch. The Americans knew what the Japanese were likely to do. They just lacked the exact times and places where the Japanese were going to strike.

The ships of Admiral Shima's force are shown on the next page.

Into the Jaws of Death

Battleship FUSO

Battleship YAMASHIRO

Cruiser MOGAMI

Destroyers ASAGUMO YAMAGUMO MICHICHIO

Destroyer SHIGURE

7 The American Plan

The American codebreakers provided the US top commanders with a lot of data about what the Japanese were planning. American cover forces were placed to prevent enemy ships from reaching the more vulnerable transports in Leyte Gulf. The major American fleet with big carriers and fast battleships was north of the Philippines where it could deal with either, or both, the Japanese squadrons approaching from Japan or the Sibuyan Sea.

The southern approach, via Surigao Strait, was to be protected by the Seventh Fleet bombardment groups. This force far outnumbered the Japanese groups that were about to attempt penetrating into the transport area. It also had superior radar and fire control, and, as noted, superb intelligence regarding Japanese intentions. The US battleships and cruisers patrolled slowly, back and forth, across the northern exit of the strait. Destroyers waited in the wings to make torpedo attacks down both sides. The stage was set for delivery of an overwhelming blow to the advancing Japanese. All that was missing was precise data on the exact location of the enemy. That would be the major job for the PT boats. The boats were to be located all around the passage to ensure detection of the approaching Japanese forces.

The entire Leyte invasion operation was covered by many war correspondents. They often pooled their stories for transmission to the US. Sometimes the exact same stories would be printed in dozens of American newspapers. The MTB squadrons had only one war correspondent that would be with them for the coming battle. Martin Sheridan, whose home paper was the Boston Globe, had been granted permission to ride along in one of the boats. He would be on board PT-132, named 'Sea Bat', for the night. Sea Bat was also the flagship boat for a trio under the command of MTB Squadron 7 commanding officer, 36 year old LCDR Robert Leeson from Brookline, MA.

8 MTBRONS Seventh Fleet

Planning for the use of MTBs had begun early. The intent was to use them as an early warning screen covering the southern approaches to the Leyte beach area. In addition, they could interdict Japanese barge traffic that might be used to reinforce the Leyte garrison. Finally, they had lots of utility missions, like VIP taxi or guerilla cooperation, that they could perform. The biggest problem seemed to be how to get them to the scene. The PTs had been based at Mios Woendi on the coast of New Guinea. Leyte was about 1200 miles away. That's about half the distance across America from coast to coast. The PT boats didn't carry nearly enough fuel to make that kind of trip. Their tenders would accompany them and provide extra fuel. The tenders could top off from fleet oilers, something the tiny PTs could not really do. CDR S. Bowling, the senior officer of the MTB squadrons in the Southwest Pacific, had been consulted about this trip. His first response was "It's too far for the boats to make in one hop, even if escorted by tenders." To this he added "The margin of safety is too thin to make this acceptable". But the top brass insisted, and Biff Bowling couldn't come up with a better plan within the given 12parameters.

PT-191 Refueling during the run from New Guinea

PT-194 refueling   NHHC 80-G-345815

---

[12] Hell on Keels 2706

Prior to departure the boats topped off their fresh water tanks and took on extra provisions. The trip began on Friday, 13 Oct. Nobody paid attention to the old sailors' superstition about departing on Friday the 13th. The voyage was made at 15 knots. There were 4 tenders and 44 MTBs, plus an Army Air Corps crash boat. The PTs refueled regularly. Each tender streamed a hose astern for one MTB while another came up alongside to starboard to take a second hose. For fueling the tenders slowed to 9 knots. Some of the fuel was contaminated and the crews of the boats had to strain it through a chamois. Even then, PT-152 experienced several occasions when her engines stopped due to fuel problems. 13The trip was exhausting for the crews. They were in dire need of a little rest time when they arrived 2 days ahead of the main landings. Nevertheless, offensive PT patrols began almost immediately.

Meanwhile, American intelligence provided the top commanders with a tremendous advantage. US codebreakers had been reading Japanese encrypted radio transmissions for most of the war The Fleet Radio Unit Pacific (FRUPac) and the Joint Intelligence Center Pacific Ocean Area (JICPOA), located side by side at

---

[13] Ibid

Makalapa, next to Pearl Harbor, in Hawaii, were able to provide translations of Japanese radio messages to the senior American leaders almost as fast as the Japanese themselves received them. The outline of the Japanese "Sho" plan was in American hands months before it was actually executed. When the landings on Leyte resulted in the Japanese sortie, The US Intelligence teams could report when the northern force departed, when the main body left Lingga Roads, near Singapore, and when the southern force weighed anchor from Brunei. All the American admirals still needed were the precise location of the enemy.

9 Enter the MTB Squadrons: preparing for battle

On the morning of 24 Oct the MTB Squadrons and their tenders were at their established mobile base locations as follows:

The overall Commander of the MTBs was 47 year old CDR Selwyn Stewart Bowling. He had been known as 'Biff' since his days at the Naval Academy where he lettered in both swimming and soccer all four years. Participation in competitive sports was considered by many to indicate the kind of personality that was needed in a PT boat officer. CDR Bowling had previously been the commander of MTBRON21. He had handpicked his boat commanders and was reported to have chosen only officers who were at least 6' tall and who had experience in team sports. As the commander of the Seventh Fleet PT boats he was assigned tactical identification CTG 70.1 (Commander, Task Group 70.1). His flagship, OYSTER BAY (AGP-6), and her sister, WILLOUGHBY (AGP-9) were at anchor in San Pedro Bay with 28 MTBs. WACHAPREAGUE (AGP-8) was at anchor in Liloan Bay with another 15 MTBs[14]. Several of her MTBs were out on patrol and on special missions on 23 October:

---

[14] Naval War College – Battle for Leyte Gulf Vol V 1958 p34

Into the Jaws of Death

PT 128 and 130 of MTBRON7 on patrol in Ormoc Bay

PT 127 and 196 on a guerilla support mission.

PT 150 and 191 of MTBRON 12 on patrol west of Leyte

PT 192 and 195 were out trying to deliver a detachment of Alamo Scouts, the Sixth Army special reconnaissance team.

These 8 boats had all returned to their tender shortly after daylight.15

Also PT 491 and 495 of MTBRON 33 were on a mission in support of guerillas at Homonhon Island. These two boats returned at 1320. 16

CDR Bowling aboard PT-369 in the Philippines
80-G-283915

---

[15] NWC p130
[16] MTBRON 33 war diary 23-24 Oct 1944

LT Donald Francis Seaman   Seventh Fleet MTBRONs Intelligence Officer

After breakfast, at around 0830, CDR Bowling, LCDR Leeson, the senior MTBRON commander and Bowling's operations officer, and LT Donald F. Seaman, his intelligence officer, were called to the CTF 77 flagship, AGC WASATCH, for a conference with CAPT Richard Harold Cruzen, the TF77 operations officer17. CAPT Cruzen noted the PTs were to be disposed "to obtain the earliest possible information of the approach of any enemy forces attempting to pass through Surigao Strait that night with the intent of a hit and run raid on the transports in the Leyte Gulf Area. The incidental purpose was to inflict early damage by PT torpedoes."18

---

[17] NWC p131

[18] NWC p131

Tenders and MTBs off Leyte prior to the battle

CDR Bowling was now informed of the expected Japanese main fleet attack on the landing area and American plans to defeat it. He returned to OYSTER BAY and began making plans accordingly.

It's interesting to point out some facts about LT Seaman. He was already 34 years old, and married, when he joined the navy. After initial training, the 5' 11" tall officer was sent to the South Pacific as the Intelligence officer for the Seventh Fleet MTBs. While that force was operating off New Guinea he volunteered to ride along in PT489 on a special mission to rescue a downed American aviator. LCDR Arthur Preston, who will be mentioned later, received the Medal of Honor for that activity. LT Seaman and another man actually dived into the water at Halmahera Island to bring the man to the boat. Seaman was awarded the Navy Cross.

At 1329, local time, on the afternoon of October 24th CDR Bowling received the expected order;

CTF 77 230419 Oct 1944 to CTG70.1 – "Station maximum number PTs lower Surigao Strait tonight. To remain south of 10- 10' North during darkness. Assigned task to report and attack enemy surface forces entering Leyte Gulf"19

Biff Bowling then issued his own orders:

CTG70.1 240504 to WACHAPREAGUE info all MTB "Expect Tokyo Express tonight. Before darkness station boats in sections of two or three each at following positions: Southwest tip of Panaon Island, south of Madilao Point, south of Limasawa island, two sections patrol between Agio Point Bohol past Camiguin Island to

---

[19] NWC p99

Sepaca Point Mindanao. Vital repeat vital each section leader report contacts and that other section leaders and WACHAPREAGUE relay these reports to CTF 77. Twenty-one boats from OYSTER BAY stationed by sections as follows: southeast Panaon Island, Bilaa Point Mindanao, in Surigao strait five sections; one off Sumilon Island, one mid-channel off Katahid Point Dinigat Island. Two off Kanihaan Island, one southeast Amagusan Point. WACHAPREAGUE inform LCIs last station. Sections attack independently after making contact report."[20]

It was sent to WACHAPREAGUE because the tenders were no longer together, and included data on where his PTs would be to avoid confusion. The LCIs were mentioned because they would have to cover the entrance to Sogod Bay since all the PTs would be busy. LT Weston Carpenter Pullen Jr., commander of MTBRON 12, was responsible for informing the LCIs, and did so when PT-172, in which he was embarked, sortied.

The OYSTER BAY squadron and boat commanders were called to the flagship for a briefing and the detailed plan was presented to them by CDR Bowling. He also instructed them that no ships moving south down the

---

[20] NWC p132

strait during or after the battle were to be attacked. This was a precaution to avoid having PTs attacking friendly forces. ENS Terry Chambers, second officer of PT 491, missed the briefing because he was off arranging for food for his crew. But as the officers returned to their boats there was soon feverish activity as the crews topped off fuel, water, food and ammunition in preparation for the coming action.

Crew members took cartons of C-Rations and stored them in the cabinets in the galley. Others put 4 round clips of 40mm projectiles in the ready racks near the after gun and loaded the ammunition magazines for the 20mm guns. There was a mix of several different rounds with colored tips on the projectiles; white meant high explosive, red was high explosive incendiary, grey was high explosive tracer, green was high explosive incendiary tracer, and a black tip was armor piercing. The fuel and fresh water tanks were topped off. Before actually departing every man aboard would don a long sleeved shirt and long trousers as well as strapping on his helmet. The boats also carried bags of saline solution to use for inter venous transfusions, and packets of sulfanilamide powder for disinfecting wounds.

The PTs would patrol in 3 boat sections in 13 areas along Surigao straight and the approaches to it as shown on the following page. All PT voice communication would be on the MTB Common circuit (3120 KHz). This kept them off the main force TBS circuit, which was, in any case, already heavily overloaded. But it was not far from the Local Air Warning and Anti-Submarine Patrol circuit that most ships with more extensive radio equipment also guarded, so it could provide the larger ships with added information indirectly.

A look at the map of the patrol areas shows that there was an advance warning line north and South of Camiguin Island, and additional patrol areas on both sides of Surigao strait from the southern entrance up to part of the strait that was intended to be a killing ground for the approaching Japanese.

CTG 70.1
October 24th

SECTION	PT'S ASSIGNED*	LOCATION
...al PT's	152, 130, 131	North half of a line from Agio Point, Bohol Island, to Sipaca Point, Mindanao Island. Midpoint: 9°-33'N, 124°-38'E
...iguis PT's	127, 128, 129	South half of a line from Agio Point, Bohol Island, to Sipaca Point, Mindanao Island. Midpoint: 9°-12'N, 124°-49'E
...sawa PT's	151, 146, 190	South of Limasawa Island. 9°-52'N, 125°-04'E
Southwest Panaon PT's	196, 150, 194	Southwest tip of Panaon Island. 9°-54'N, 125°-15'E
Madilao Point PT's	192, 191, 195	Madilao Point, Mindanao Island. 9°-45'N, 125°-23'E
Southeast Panaon PT's	134, 132, 137	Southeast tip of Panaon Island. 9°-55'N, 125°-15'E
Bilaa Point PT's	494, 497, 324	Bilaa Point, Mindanao Island. 9°-49'N, 125°-25'E
Sumilon PT's	523, 524, 526	South of Sumilon Island. 9°-54'N, 125°-26'E
Lower Surigao PT's	490, 491, 493	Midway between Kanhatid Point, Dinagat Island and Panaon Island. 10°-05'N, 125°-22'E
Upper Surigao PT's	327, 321, 326	4 miles west of Kanihaan Island. 10°-10'N, 125°-24'E
Kanihaan PT's	495, 489, 492	South of Kanihaan Island. 10°-10'N, 125°-28'E
South Amagusan Point PT's	320, 330, 331	South of Amagusan Point, Leyte. 10°-14'N, 125°-15'E
East Amagusan Point PT's	328, 323, 329	2 miles east of Amagusan Point, Leyte. 10°-15'N, 125°-17'E

* OTC in first listed PT.

21

---

21 NWC p135

The idea that a possible major action was imminent spread quickly as the crews made sure their boats were fully fueled and armed. Some squadron members were not part of the crews going out on patrol. PHM2c William Edward Gaffney Jr was one of them. Gaffney was a medical corpsman and the PT boat crews were not fitted with facilities for handling casualties. But all squadron personnel had at least some minimal training in every job on board, Gaffney asked to be added to the men on PT-493 and the skipper, LT Bill Brown, agreed. Brown also added 2 other extra men to his crew. One of them was diminutive LTJG Richard Airth Hamilton. Hamilton was all of 5'7" tall and weighed in at about 140 pounds. His small size had not kept him from playing rugby in his native state of North Dakota. His fierce competitive and aggressive spirit had apparently resulted in something that caused his temporary removal from his original boat position. It also got him the nickname of "Dickie Dare", taken from a contemporary heroic comic book figure. Dickie Dare Hamilton convinced Bill Brown to let him ride along as third officer. Staying behind when there was a chance of serious combat was something no PT sailor wanted, least of all Hamilton. The overall attitude of the PT sailors was summed up well by QM3 Thomas Edward ('Tom') Tenner of PT-127:" We were afraid of nothing".

The scene on the WACHAPREAGUE to the south was similar. "We were signaled to come in, refuel, and rearm," said PT-127 RM2c John Michael ('Jake') Hanley. "We had a big mission coming up that night. "

MTBRON 7 commander, LCDR Leeson, briefed his officers about their duties, pointing to locations of reported Japanese forces on maps mounted on plywood boards.

"Our assignment on this mission is to supply intelligence reports on their advance and strength", he told his boat commanders "Use all precautions and don't fire at our own PTs. Grab a sandwich in the wardroom and proceed to your positions as quickly as possible. Good Luck, men."22

In the afternoon before the mission the Japanese had mounted a major air attack on the American ships involved in the landing. A pair of enemy aircraft was detected heading toward the OYSTER BAY. The tender sounded the General Quarters alarm, her crew went to Battle stations, and all the PTs were ordered to clear away from her sides. Antiaircraft fire seems to have quickly downed one of the Japanese intruders and its

---

22

The Times-Tribune (Scranton, Pennsylvania) · 25 Nov 1944, Sat · Page

companion joined it in the sea a few minutes later.
Within a few hours all the operational mosquito boats
were beginning to head for their night time patrol areas.
Between 1520 and 1535 all OYSTER BAY PTs departed
for their assigned stations. WACHAPREAGUE boats
started out at 1730 and were all en route by 1830.

After the PTs departed Biff Bowling received a message
from his boss. CTF77 240609 "Insure enemy forces do
not repeat do not pass undetected through strait
between Dinigat Island and Mindanao"

This prompted him to tell WACHAPREAGUE (CTG70.1
240933) "deliver following message to COMRON 36 and
PeeTee 494. Plain language. Keep watch on passage to
east of you as well as one to west"

Weather was typical for Philippines during SE monsoon
season with temperatures varying only a few degrees in
the 80 degree Fahrenheit range (about 27 degrees
Celsius) and high humidity. There was a lot of haze,
cloud, and many rain squalls of short duration resulting
in limited range for visual detection at night. Nightfall
didn't result in much change. In an age without air-
conditioning, that was fairly uncomfortable. Sailors
went about their normal routine work wearing cut-off
trousers and undershirts. Often, even the shirts were

discarded. But for a combat sortie the crew wore long pants and long sleeved shirts and put on their steel helmets. They dressed for battle in order to help limit casualties.

Fuel tanks were filled to full capacity, s were fresh water tanks. Ready ammunition for every gun was also set at fully loaded condition. Reserve magazines were completely filled up. All the clip racks around the 40mm gun aft had full 4 round clips in them.

The pilothouse was prepared with the latest, up to date, communications information. This included daily visual challenge and responses as well as the standard code books. On many boats these were written on a display board inside the pilothouse. The radios were checked for tuning to the proper frequency. Very likely, the combat sortie checklist included cleaning the insulators on the base of the antennas from possible salt encrustation that might affect reception.

The routine also meant having the navigation charts for the area laid out and that there were pencils, and spares, readily available. No one going into potential combat wants to find that some item he needs has not been checked or is not in the place where he expects it to be.

PT-130   Navsource 120513005

10 Bohol PTs First Contact PT-152 PT-130 PT-131

Group 1, which was under the command of COMMTBRON 12, LT Weston Carpenter Pullen Jr. from Norwich CONN, left their home tender, USS WACHAPREAGUE, for patrol at 1810. Their station was off Bohol, at the southern end of Surigao Strait. Pullen rode in PT-152 for this mission. PT-152, whose name, 'Lack-a Nooky', was painted on the front of the pilot house. She was commanded by LTJG Joseph Albert Eddins, a native of Roswell, NM. The name of the boat comes from a slang term referring to not having sex, a status that was all too common for PT sailors in the South Pacific. Eddins had only recently taken over as skipper of PT-152. During the long voyage from Mios Woendi he had been the Executive Officer of PT-195. The other boats in the section were PT-130, 'New Guinea Krud', commanded by 25 year old LTJG Ian Duncan ('Mal') Malcolm from Cambridge MA, and PT-131, 'TARFU', commanded by 23 year old LTJG Peter Robert Gadd Jr. from Sacramento CA. TARFU is an acronym popular in the military during the war meaning "Things Are Really Fucked Up". The crews, like the boat skippers, came from all over the United States. What they had in common was their youth. The officers were mostly in their mid to early 20s. Crew members ranged in age from 18 to 28.

PT-130 cockpit Navsource 120513003

PT-131 Navsource 120513104 from Michael Owen

PT-130   NH 80-G-326349 Navsource 120513008

PT-131 - Note 5" rocket launchers forward and extra twin 0.50 cal. aft of torpedo. 80-G-345819

PT-132 cockpit Navsource 120515203

The 3 boats reached a position 3 away on miles bearing
050 from Agio Point at 2035 and began patrolling on

course 169, speed 12 knots, with closed mufflers. The primary sensor for search was radar. Visual search was limited by both the darkness and the frequent rain squalls that passed through the area all night. The straits were wider than the maximum effective range of the type SO radar they carried. That meant the section had to travel back and forth to ensure coverage of the entire area. They sailed in formation, echeloned to the left with PT-152 as guide in position ahead and on the starboard side. The distance between boats was 75 yards.

The first contact came from the radar operator on PT-130. He picked up 2 blips on his boats' starboard quarter about 10 miles away at 2215. The section was close to 18 miles from Bohol Island at the time. The section reversed course to 345 and increased speed to 24 knots in order to close the target blips. The commanding officer of PT-130, Mal Malcolm described the feeling at that time.

"At 10:30 that night we got our initial contact with the force and we reversed our course to head them off. We wanted particularly their course and speed to radio to the base. We weren't particularly nervous then – no more so than on regular patrols when we run in under shore guns and sink a barge. It's like waiting for the kickoff in a football game. There's no sport in the world like closing within 50 yards of a barge and literally blowing it apart. But this was no barge fight. We were moving along easily with all guns manned when I looked over the port beam and saw two cruisers bearing down on us. A destroyer was just crossing our bow. They were heading right for us all right."23

At 2230 PT-152 also acquired the targets on radar and began tracking them within the limited capabilities of the PT boat's radar installation. The first blip, directly ahead, resolved itself into 2 separate targets. The other, bearing about 10 degrees to the left remained a single target. They contacts seemed to be heading on course 080 at about 25 knots. As the section closed, the enemy resolved into 5 separate contacts, 2 large ships, which were actually the Japanese battleships FUSO and YAMASHIRO, and a screen of 3 smaller vessels. The Japanese force was actually on course 065 at 18 knots at that time. The section slowed to 10 knots and engaged mufflers. In PT-152 the radio operator, 19 year old James Johnston Dempster, was making repeated, and unsuccessful, attempts to get out a contact report. Blonde, grey eyed, Dempster had reported to MTBRON 12 the previous April. His impression was that the

---

[23] Boston Globe report Thursday Nov 9th, 1944 page 1 and 4

Japanese were jamming their operating frequency. The section was still too far away to effectively launch torpedoes, and the enemy was certain to detect them soon, either visually, or with radar.

Sure enough, at 2252 Japanese destroyer SHIGURE reported "3 MTBs sighted bearing 30 degrees true". At 2254 the Japanese began to maneuver towards the irritating mosquito boats. Following their own doctrine, they turned toward the Americans and opened fire. At 2300 the Japanese admiral ordered SHIGURE to illuminate. The destroyer attempted to locate their enemies using both searchlights and star shells.

"I had just radioed the other boats'" LTJG Malcolm continued, "When the cruisers opened up on us with eight inch and four-point-seven inch guns. A dozen star shells burst over our heads. At the same time they pinned each boat with a searchlight and it was bright as daylight. From then on, brother, we weren't scared. We were terror stricken."24

The gunfire was more accurate than either side realized at the time. One 4.7" shell from Japanese destroyer SHIGURE hit PT-130 and went completely through her wooden hull forward without exploding. Others

---

24 ibid

exploded in the water about 20 yards off the starboard bow of PT-152. She was hit by a lot of shrapnel. Eighteen year old TM3c Robert Michael Clarkin from Jersey City was topside. "The first I remembered was the boat hauling ass away. We hadn't fired torpedoes and we were caught in a searchlight. The noise was incredible", Clarkin said later.25

Clarkin, who was called Bob by his shipmates, was 6 feet tall. He heard an explosion and glanced forward.

"Charlie Midgett, the guy on the bow thirty-seven millimeter gun was down. He looked pretty bad to me. "Bob said, "He probably died right away".26

Charlie was 21 year old Charles Francois Midgett from North Carolina. He was the 37mm gunner forward on PT-152. He was a MoMM3c whose normal job would have been in the engine room. But PT sailors often were able to handle assignments not related to their 'official' ratings. A Japanese shell had exploded directly above his gun. The gun had been tossed off of its mount. The wooden deck around the mount was riddled with little holes from the shrapnel scattered by the enemy shell when it burst. Midgett was seriously wounded. The

---

[25] Voices p 105
[26] Ibid

loader, 18 year old S1c Rufus Everett Malone Jr., the boat's cook, was stunned by the blast. His eardrums were perforated and he suffered from a concussion and shock as well as facial burns. The 2 injured crew members were taken below where the Executive Officer, LTJG Lawrence E. Johnson tried to deal with their wounds.

The following picture shows where the gun Midgett manned had been located.

Navsource PT-152 Navsource 120515201 from 80-G-345122

"Some of the guys carried Charlie and a couple of wounded down to the skipper's cabin." Clarkin related.

Red hot shell fragments penetrated into the crew compartment of PT-152. Bedding was set on fire. Blue eyed Bob Clarkin spent about 5 minutes putting out the fire. Clarkin, incidentally, was normally part of the crew of PT-191. He was aboard PT-152 to fill in for a missing crew member.

"The mattresses in crew's quarters were burning, so I went below and hauled them up and tossed them over the side." He said.27.

PT-152 swiftly turned to starboard, increased speed back to 24 knots and began zigzagging to avoid enemy fire. The smoke generator was activated, but it failed to provide any relief. The Japanese seemed to use the smoke as an aiming point and their searchlights, that had been temporarily extinguished when Lack-a-Nooky's guns had started firing at them, were once again illuminating the scene. GM3c Frank Alexander Miller and S1c Earl Harris Jr. had tried to open the Titanium tetrachloride smoke generator. Now they tried to shut it down, but were unsuccessful. They were rewarded with hand and facial burns from the gas and

---

[27] Voices p 105

shrapnel wounds from enemy gunfire. They unceremoniously dumped the apparatus over the side. The engagement continued for over 20 minutes; the PT trying to escape, and the Japanese chasing them. LTJG Joe Eddins watched the Japanese and whenever he saw a gun flash he made a radical alteration of course. Each turn was made at random, to avoid following a predictable pattern. At the same time as the first Japanese shells landed LT Pullen ordered his other boats, PTs 130 and 131 to close the Caminguin group to ensure the contact report would get through. This resulted in the separation of the group, because the Caminguin group was located to the north.

PT-130 turned across the stern of PT-152 and operated her own smoke generator using a home-built remote lever that was located alongside the helm. Using this improvised control system PT-130 was able to lay intermittent bursts of smoke to help cover both PT-152 and her own withdrawal.

A large caliber Japanese shell, possibly a 4.7" from the cruiser Mogami, hit PT-130. It slammed into the warhead of the forward port torpedo. The warhead was cracked open and approximately a quarter of the TNT inside was scattered about without exploding. The Japanese projectile continued forward, shearing off the leg of the recently installed port rocket launcher. Then it tore a path about 10 feet long and 2 feet wide through the wooden deck. It smashed up 9 deck beams and 8 hull frames on its way through the forward crew compartment. The shell exited just above the chine near the bulkhead separating the crews head and their sleeping quarters without ever exploding.

LTJG Ian Malcolm described it like this: "The initial salvo was right on us. They were throwing six round salvoes every 12 seconds and that kept up for the next 25 minutes. On the fourth salvo an armor piercing shell slammed into us, tearing the warhead and casing off a torpedo, ripping through the deck and filling every compartment below with torpedo TNT. You could pick it up by the handful. 28"

"The fish's detonator cap was hanging by a wire. I dove for it, but one of the gunner's mates got there first, tossed the detonator cap to me, and I batted it over the side." Mal said.29

Remarkably, no one was injured and Mal Malcolm's PT-130 was able to continue without any further problems except for her radios not being functional.

Boston Globe report Thursday Nov 9th, 1944 page 1 and 4[28]
[29] Voices p 106

A searchlight on SHIGURE illuminated PT-152 and in response her 40mm gun fired some 60 rounds at it. One of the twin 50 cal. machine guns emptied both 200 round ready boxes of bullets at the same target. The searchlight was soon switched off. There was no indication that the PT gunfire was the cause, but Joe Eddins would later remark "Return 40mm fire made the enemy reluctant to continue use of searchlight."30

"The skipper signaled me to roll one of the stern depth charges" said Bob Clarkin.31

The action report noted that two depth charges set for 100 feet were actually rolled off the side in the hope that their explosion would confuse the Japanese. In addition, the boats gunners opened fire on the searchlights, hoping to extinguish them and escape from the accurate Japanese gunfire.32

From PT-130 that sequence of events looked like this to Ian Malcolm.

---

[30] The Hooligan Navy
[31] Voices p 106
[32] Action report, PT-152, night of 24/25 October 1944, p 2

"The fifth salvo hit the section leader boat commanded by LCDR Weston C. Pullen of Connecticut. It started a small fire and blew hell out of the bow"33.

Another Japanese projectile had exploded to starboard and caused the starboard Packard engine to cease operating. Immediately, another 6 foot tall sailor, MoMM1c Lloyd Lester Greenup, a 28 year old from Montana who was in charge of the engine room, went into action. He restarted the engine and his boat continued at full power.

Her radios were completely disabled, although the crew did not recognize this for several minutes. Being under enemy fire can be distracting, to say the least.

PT-152 came about in order to try to reach an attack position. But after less than an hour the commander recognized that his radios were not functioning, and he was not closing on the Japanese. PT-152 broke off the action and headed for home. There was hope that they could get medical aid for their badly wounded shipmate. It was not to be. Charles Midgett died on board his boat at about 0100 that morning.

---

[33] Boston Globe report Thursday Nov 9th, 1944 page 1 and 4

Into the Jaws of Death

Aboard PT-130 skipper Mal Malcolm watched his section leader in PT-152 heading back towards the Japanese.

"The Japs followed the smoke as it lifted and began throwing shells again. Pullen's radio was out, but he messaged that he was all right and to try to reach Cady's group and get the report through." Mal said.34

"I set course for Cady and the last thing I saw was Pullen opening up with his 40-millimeter. I figured then he was gone and the firing was his last ditch stand. But as it turned out, he got away and was firing to distract their attention from me. That did it, and they turned from me to chase Pullen. He and the other boat slipped around in back of them and followed them up the Mindanao Sea to Surigao Strait."35

"Our only chance was to run. There was no chance of a torpedo shot at that range and we still hadn't been able to report to base. The Japs were jamming our radio. They were listening to us and Cady's section on the other side of the channel and they knew our boat numbers as well as we did."

---

[34] Boston Globe, Thurs Nov 9th 1944 - page 2
[35] ibid

PT-130 and PT-131 sighted the other group of 3 MTBs they were seeking to join at about 2350. They were located some 3 miles north of Camiguin Island. Mal Malcolm drove his boat, New Guinea Krud, alongside PT-127 and leapt across to get his bosses contact report relayed up the chain of command. He was somewhat shaken by the experience up to then. He put it this way, "We had been under cruiser fire for 25 minutes and when I got aboard Cady's boat I couldn't talk sense and he had to shake it out of me and radio it to base." 3637

Jake Hanley on PT-127 remembered it slightly differently. "We moved bow to bow with the 130 and Malcolm came aboard. We crowded into the chartroom. Ian was pretty excited. But Cady was a man who could calm anyone down. Cady took down Malcolm's information. I got the code book and converted the information into coded groups of four or five letters to transmit by voice on the radio. I had to repeat the code groups over and over before I got an acknowledgement. I could tell the Japanese were trying to scramble the signal, but I finally got a confirmation."38

---

[36] Boston Globe, Thurs Nov 9th 1944 - page 2

[38] Voices

The relay was successful. The groups' primary mission had been accomplished.

"We picked them up about 6 in the morning again." Said Ian Malcolm, "But we were all nearly out of torpedoes. We had let most everything go in the night. But we let them have what was left and then they were gone."39

All five boats (127, 128, 129, 130, and 131) remained together until about 0321, when PT-130 and PT-131 were left patrolling while the others moved away and then lay to for a little over 2 hours. At 0545 all 5 boats joined together again and. at 0606 they set course for Liloan Bay to return to their tender.

LT Weston Carpenter Pullen Jr.   1962 visa photo

---

39 Delaplane Boston Globe 9 Nov 1944

PT-152 SC3c Rufus Everett Malone findagrave.com

11 Camiguin PTs PT-127, PT-128, PT-129

The first line of MTB patrols was the trip wire line that stretched across the Mindanao Sea between Agio Point on Bohol and Camiguin Island and continued on to Bipaca Point on Mindanao. It was split between two groups of PTs. The northwest section was covered by 3 boats from MTBRON 7. PT-127 carried the section commander, 24 year old LTJG John Atwood Cady. The skipper of the boat was another 24 year old, ENS Dudley Jay Johnson from Texas. Johnson had been the second officer on the boat from January, 1944 until October 22nd, when he took over as commanding officer of the boat. Cady had been the boat commanding officer at that time. Jack Cady would soon complete a tour of 18 months overseas and be rotated back to the MTB Training Center in Melville, Rhode Island.

Johnson and Cady had been a popular, and effective, team when running PT-127. QM3c Tom Tenner described them like this, "We didn't like our first executive officer, so he had to go. We got Dudley Johnson to replace him. He and the skipper, Jack Cady, were great. They listened and when we needed something we went to them. They didn't go for this ordering and demanding way of getting things done".40

The first XO appears to have been ENS Howard Green, who was later XO on PT-134.

Dudley Johnson had been a student at Texas A&M before he joined the navy. He was tall (5' 11'') but slight, weighing only 148 pounds. Johnson with his strong Texas accent, made a sharp contrast to the new XO, Edmund Mcnamara, from South Boston. Being just over 6 feet tall and weighing in at over 200 pounds, was ample reason for Mcnamara to be nicknamed 'Big Ed' at Holy Cross University where he starred in football for 3 years and played well in a wide variety of positions; end, tackle, and fullback. After the war, Mcnamara went on to be an FBI agent, and later, Boston Police Commissioner.

PT-127 was the oldest boat in Squadron 7. In October, 1942, she had traveled to Norfolk, VA, where she was loaded aboard USS MONONGAHELA (AO-42). A type T2-A-MC-K fleet oiler, and taken to the Panama Canal. After a short stay there the boat was one of several carried to Brisbane on deck in special cradles on SS WHITE PLAINS. From there, MTBRON 7 moved to Milne

---

40 Voices p 68

Bay on the southeastern tip of New Guinea from where they really began engaging the Japanese. All the boats of MTBRON7 were painted in green camouflage.

PTs en route to the South Pacific
USNHHC 80-G-184393

The boats in the photo are actually from MTBRON 9, not 7 but the ship is SS WHITE PLAINS, a civilian Maritime Commission type T2-SE-A1 tanker.

When PT-127 left the USA she was armed with the standard outfit for the first set of Elco 80 foot PTs. That meant she had four torpedo tubes with the older Mark VIII surface torpedoes that were launched using a propelling charge of black powder. She also had a limited gun armament of a 20mm gun aft and 2 twin 0.50 caliber machineguns in gun tubs on the port and starboard side. That would soon change.

Field modifications to PT armament started during the Guadalcanal-Solomons campaign when early PTs encountered Japanese landing barges used for resupplying the enemy garrisons. The barges were too small to warrant use of a torpedo, and the existing PT gun armament at the time was not very effective. Larger caliber guns were needed. One PT got an army 37mm anti-tank gun and tied it down on the Elco boats expansive forward deck. It was aimed by pointing the bow of the boat at the target just before firing. The PT crews were aware that there was a lot of space forward where extra weapons could be mounted. Army Air Corps P-39 fighters had operated from the Guadalcanal airfield. The P-39s had a 37mm cannon designed to fire through the propeller hub. One of these was adapted to a mount on the bow of the 80' Elco and was very successful. The Elco manufacturers began to add the bow gun to their production designs using 37mm guns built by an Oldsmobile plant. The 20mm gun aft was re-located to a site on the port side forward of the pilot house and an army Bofors 40mm gun was installed aft where the 20mm had previously been. The new 40mm guns came from different sources. MTBRON 12 got theirs from the Army. MTBRON 21 received theirs from The Royal Australian Army.

All the boats of MTBRON 7 had been given an overhaul and armament update during February-March, 1943. This included repainting in green camouflage. It also included replacing their older torpedo tubes with the newer side-launching installation and Mark XIII torpedoes. The weight saved made it possible to put on more guns. The overhaul involved upgrading their entire gun armament. When completed, the boats sported a 37mm on the bow, a 40mm astern, and the 20mm relocated forward. The twin fifties in the gun tubs also now had flash hiders on their muzzles.

MoMM2c Donald Frederick Bujold from Michigan was another typical example of how PT sailors often worked at jobs that were not part of their 'official' training. Don Bujold would normally have been assigned to the engine room. But, as he told it, "When they gave us the forty millimeter, I knew the gunner's mate assigned to it couldn't hit the broad side of a barn. I told Cady if I couldn't shoot any better than him I'd turn in my ticket. He said 'Okay, we'll find out.' So they put a bunch of oil drums out in the water and the skipper maneuvered the boat while I tried to hit them. Now I'd shot a few rabbits and pheasants in my day back in Michigan. I had Jake training the gun for me while I handled elevation. I knew enough to fire on the up roll of the boat and I ended up hitting the drums pretty well. So Cady told me 'The gun's all yours.'"41

Cady was LTJG John Atwood Cady, the skipper of PT-127 at the time, and now section commander. Jake was RM2c John Michael Hanley, the PT-127 radioman who was also permanently assigned as part of the 40mm gun crew.

QM3 Tom Tenner, who had joined PT-127 at the same time as Bujold, said "When the forty was installed we thought we were a battleship, that's the way it was."42

Blue eyed Thomas Edward Tenner from Pittsburgh was stationed in the chartroom. His attitude exemplified that of many PT crewmen. "We were afraid of nothing that moved. If something happened at night, we would come back disappointed if we hadn't seen it. If we saw

---

41 Voices p67-68
42 Voices p68

light, any movement on the radar, anything, we would tear right into it."43

PT-129 Sep 1942   Navsource 120512901

PT-127 LTJG Edmund Leo Mcnamara   family photo

---

43 Voices p67

PT-127 GM3c Robert James Douglas, who joined after Surigao battle.

PT-127 LTJG John A Cady Wichita Beacon Sat 25 1944

The other 2 boats patrolling this sector were PT-128 and PT-129. PT-128 under ENS Gregory J Azarigian got her name, 'Tug Boat Annie', from a story in the Saturday Evening Post that became a 1933 MGM movie of the same name starring Wallace Beery and Marie Dressler. The Skipper, whose family came to the US from Turkish ruled Armenia, had been her XO previously. He was an MIT graduate and had earned a Silver Star medal for swimming ashore in New Guinea to rescue a downed Australian airman. After the war he changed his name, legally, to the Americanized version of his Armenian name Gregory Jacob Azarigian. The second officer on 'Tug Boat Annie' was ENS H. F. Norton.

PT-128 F2c Robert J Owen   PT-129.org

PT-129 ENS Alfred Dix Leeson   Harvard yearbook

PT-128 in camouflage   Navsource 120512801

PT-128 F1c Leonard Victor Shuster on the left with an unidentified crew member

PT-129 was named 'Artful Dodger' after a character in Dickens novel Oliver Twist. Her skipper was ENS Alfred Dix Leeson. He was from a different part of Boston. At 6' 3", he was slightly taller than Mcnamara of PT-127. Leeson's father had made a good living from the lumber business he had started, and was able to afford to send his son to Harvard. Young Leeson was no stranger to small boats. He had received a sailing sloop from his father when he graduated from high school. His brother, Robert Leeson, was the Commander of MTBRON 7 and in charge of a different three boat section.

The sea was calm as the boats departed from their tender to head for their assigned patrol area. They left a wake of white water behind even though they were not proceeding at high speed. It wasn't all reflected moonlight. The tropical waters in the Philippines abounded in small sea creatures that actually emitted their own light. The phenomenon is called bioluminescence. Fireflies are a more familiar expression of this for most Americans.

The 3 boats of the section arrived on station in the center of their patrol area at about 2145. The boats lay to and began a radar watch in rotation. PT-128 was assigned the 2200-2400 watch. That watch, and the visual watches on all three boats failed to make any solid contacts throughout the night.

In the chartroom of PT-127 QM Tom Tenner waited for his turn on the radar watch. The regular radioman aboard the PT 127 would have been assigned to radar watch but he wanted to stay topside when the shooting started in an expected battle with the Japanese, instead of remaining below deck in the cabin with radar. The boat's captain granted the request "Don't worry about it, Tenner will do it."

Tenner, himself, later said "I was more than happy to learn radar, because in addition to dead reckoning navigation, I was able to see where we were going. Radar was tricky then, but I learned the tricks, and it helped me immensely. So, I had radar, and that was the biggest deal in the world."

Working the radar on the 127 Boat, Tom Tenner had simple instructions: 'Spot anything and to try to figure out where it was, what speed, and what direction.' After we did that, if we had any time left, we were supposed to attack."

But because of what he saw on radar, the PT 127 orders were changed to one of tracking and following. He had been first to find blips on radar that revealed the Japanese fleet's approach, and with the radioman's relay of his information, they found themselves providing directions to the senior admiral with the American battleships.

Tenner told a later interviewer; "I said, 'There's two battleships, two heavy cruisers.' All these little blips, and here I am, I'm a 21-year-old kid, and I was saying, 'Oh, and there are two battleships and five destroyers.' ". He recalls, "They had said 'speed, direction and following.' At the time, I got a couple more readings, and we were told, 'Keep on them, don't attack.'"

Tenner's interview continued: "That was when the PT boats found out for sure they were no match for battleships. But we attacked, fouled them up like crazy. They dropped flares. We were an annoyance to them that night. We were a big annoyance, and slowed them down. But our destroyers finished throwing their torpedoes at them, then the battleships - they had them in a 'T.' It was awful for the Japanese."

The enemy fleet was not actually in sight. What was seen were star shells and lights north of Caminguin at around 10 minutes before midnight. Because he believed this to be evidence of the presence of Japanese forces, the section commander in PT-127 tried to make a contact report. Repeated attempts to pass on the report by radio were unsuccessful. The junior boats let the section commander work at making a contact report and contented themselves with staying in company. The result was that this section neither actually sighted nor engaged the enemy during the battle.

PT-127 was frustrated by their inability to get a confirmation of their radio contact report. The boat head north to try to find another boat that could relay the report. They found LTJG 'Mal' Malcolm's PT-130.

 "Mal, are you scared?" Cady shouted by megaphone from PT 127 as boats 130 and 131 approached.

"Hell, no!" Malcolm yelled from PT 130. "I'm terrified!" 44

Malcom came aboard PT-127 in order to get a full briefing, and then returned to his own boat where he managed to send out the relayed contact report at 5 minutes after midnight. The boats returned to their patrol station until 0320 when they separated. PT-128 and PT-129 headed off on course 035 at 9kts with muffled engines. Forty minutes later they lay to on their patrol station. At 0515 they headed back to join the other section and after that, at about 0615, moved out on course 030 at 27 knots to head for their home base.

---

44 Wooden boats

PT-128 Michael Owen   Navsource
020512802

Tom Tenner's wife joined him at a reunion of PT sailors some years later. She told them "Up until this point, I thought Tom won the war all by himself - now I find he had help".

Other members of the crew of PT-127 were:

MoMM1c Ernest Carl Bohn, age 30, from Detroit, MI

MoMM2c Marvin Pettus (Pat') Horton, age 28, from Birmingham, Al

Into the Jaws of Death

MoMM2c William Frank Fisler, age 23, from
Schenectady, NY

MoMM2c Frederick Purnell, age 28, from Akron, OH

MoMM3c John William Kendig Jr., age 32, from NY, NY

F1c Ralph Anthony Ammirati, age 19, from Brooklyn, NY

QM3c Richard William Dilg, age 19, from Albany, NY

GM2c James Henry Hart, age 22,from Albany, NY

GM3c Charles Aberham Heck, age 19, from
Cleveland,OH

TM2c Lyman Albert Schoffstall, age 21 from Harrisburg,
PA

S1c Charles Raymond Horton,age 32, from Cleveland,
OH

S1c Robert Martin Greis, age 18, from Highland Park,MI

S2c Harold Paul Bruni, age 20, from Gloucester, MA

SC3c Drew Whitehead, age 22, from Sioux City, IA

PT-127 GM3c Charles A. (Chuck') Heck posing with Tommy gun pt127.org.

Right PT-127 SC3c Drew Whitehead ~1940 ancestry.com

12 Limasawa PTs PT-151, PT-146, PT-190

LTJG Dwight H Owen, nicknamed 'Swede', was riding in PT-151 as the commander of the section headed for a stretch of water south of Limasawa Island. His section consisted of PT-190, PT-146, and PT-151.

PT-151 LTJG Dwight Hall Owen HS photo   ancestry.com

PT-146 was known as 'Lucky Lady', and carried painted version of a dark haired woman alongside that name on the boats' windscreen above her number. The number actually appeared on the front of the pilot house. ENS Buford Maine Grosscup from Lincoln, Nebraska, was the skipper of the 'Lucky Lady'. PT-190, under the command of ENS Edward Stanley Haugen, a 24 year old

Californian, 45was known as 'Jack O'Diamonds'. ENS
John M Ladd commanded PT-151. 46

PT-146   Navsource 120514607

He had two other new officers in the pilot house to
assist him; ENS Glenn Martin and ENS Robert Smith (not
to be confused with another Robert Smith stationed in
the engine room)47. The boat was known in the
squadron as 'Wuncanitesenuf'. PT-190 was also carrying
an extra officer, LTJG Harold E Simon, whose departure
for the South Pacific had been delayed while he
attended Communications School. Her regular second

---

45 Muster roll MTRRON12
46 Action Report PT151
47 Action report PT151

officer was ENS Anthony Koenings from Minnesota.48 Another new arrival was Emile Jake Dath Jr. who had reported in on 8 Oct. He had participated in sail racing while in high school and was nicknamed 'E. J'. He would be learning to be a gunner's mate

PT-151 GM3c Emile Jake Dath Jr – 1942 HS photo ancestry.com

The trio got underway at 1730 and arrived on station an hour later, when it was still daylight, and lay to. They commenced a visual and radar search. Throughout the entire action the team of 20 year old RM2c John Patrick Frayne from Atlantic City, NJ, and S1c Robert Alfred Blenderman, from Sioux City, IA, kept a constant stream

---

48 Action report PT146

of radar data flowing to the officers in charge.49
Blenderman had only joined the crew 2 weeks earlier.

PT-151 RM3c Robert Alfred Blenderman HS photo
ancestry.com

After some 5 hours their boring situation was about to
change. Section commander Dwight Owen described it
like this; "At approximately 2330 the prologue began.
Off to the southwest over the horizon we saw distant
flashes of gunfire, star shells bursting and far-off sweep
of searchlights. The display continued about 15 minutes,
then blacked out. Squalls came and went. One moment
the moon shone bright as day and the next you couldn't
make out the bow of your boat. Then the radar
developed the sort of pips you read about."50 The radar
contact was in the same direction that the lights had
been seen, and at a range of approximately 9 miles.

---

49 Action Report PT151
50Bulkeley - At Close Quarters – p 383

Owen turned his section toward the contact and closed at 17 knots with mufflers engaged. PT-146 and PT-190 were located to port, and slightly forward, of PT-151's port beam.[51] The radar on board Lucky Lady" was not functioning at this time.[52]

Visual contact was made after about 20 minutes. The targets were identified as a Japanese battleship accompanied by a light cruiser and three destroyers. The enemy ships were some 2 miles ahead. The section slowed to 9 knots and continued to approach the Japanese from the port quarter of the enemy ships.

At 0010 a Japanese ship turned on a searchlight and swept the area to starboard of the approaching PTs. Three minutes later another searchlight winked on from almost dead ahead. At 0015 the order was given to launch torpedoes.
PT-151 was only carrying 2 fish on this mission. The other 2 torpedo locations were occupied by depth charges. The starboard torpedo was sent on its' way toward the enemy battleship. But the torpedo man on the port side failed to hear the order. For the next minute and a half the boat tried to regain a good firing position, but was illuminated by the beam of a

---

[51] Action Report PT151
[52] Action Report pT146

searchlight from an enemy destroyer that was located astern of the battleship. Boo Grosscup in PT-146 had 2 new crew members on board; TM3 Clifford Edward Cook and S1c (GM) Edwin Wallace Coburn, known as Wally to his shipmates. Wally Coburn manned the port 0.50 machine guns and emptied his ready ammunition boxes shooting at the searchlights. PT-146 also launched her starboard torpedo at a range of 1800 yards, but it was seen to run erratically, turning left about 90 degrees immediately after launch[53].

As PT-146 turned left to prepare for a second torpedo shot the searchlight beam caught the other two boats. The skipper of PT-146 had been a star basketball player in high school. It earned him a scholarship to Doane College where he met his future wife. They were married just after he completed the course for new officers at Newport, RI. Now Grosscup tried to get in position for another shot. He told his exec, ENS Joe Campbell, to order the stern 40mm to hold off shooting while he made the approach. Campbell called to the gunner "Hold your Fire!" The gunner didn't hear the whole order. The engine room intake was located between his position and ENS Campbell. There was too much noise for Campbell's voice to be heard clearly. The

---

[53] Action report PT146

word "Fire" did get through, and that was what the gunner did. The flash from the 40mm gave the Japanese a target. Very quickly PT-146 was bracketed by 4 shells from Japanese guns. A Japanese searchlight caught "Lucky Lady" directly in its beam. Skipper Grosscup spun the wheel hard to starboard and opened the throttles on all engines to full power. The second torpedo wasn't launched. What saved the boat was a rain squall that dropped a lot of water on her just at that moment. It obscured the boat's movements and allowed her to get away safely.

PT-146 ENS Buford Maine Grosscup as midshipman – ancestry.com

PT-151 also turned sharply to the right in order to withdraw. PT-146 and PT-190 both opened fire on the searchlight with their own guns as the boats passed Swede Owen's flagship, going in opposite directions. That searchlight was soon turned off. But the battleships' light still kept illuminating the 'Wuncanitesenuf'. PT-190 only managed to get off 2 rounds from her 40mm gun and 5 from the forward mounted 37mm before both jammed. GM2c Clarence Pool, a 5' 11" Texan, and GM3c Edwin Gerald Hutcheson, a nineteen year old from Elmira, New York, managed to restore their weapons to working order, but were unable to resume firing.

On PT-151, ENS Ladd was zig-zagging as one of his men raced aft to open the smoke generator cylinder.GM3c Russell Eugene Simmons, a 5' 8" teenager from Robison, Illinois, was in the port side twin 0.50 turret mount. He emptied both the 250 round ammunition boxes on his guns firing at the searchlights. Of course, the tracers from his guns also gave the Japanese a position for aiming their own guns, and Simmons was oblivious to anything else around him beyond firing at the Japs. ENS Ladd realized what was happening and moved off the bridge to get his port gunner to stop shooting. Russ Simmons wasn't responding. Ladd beat him on the helmet and shoulders to get his attention. That was just when an enemy projectile exploded nearby. A piece of shrapnel hit the gunner's helmet and knocked him senseless. Blue eyed Seaton Shepherd was nearby.

PT-151 S1c Seaton Grantland Shepherd- ancestry.com

"They got Si, They got Si", he yelled.54

Simmons heard this and stood up. He ran his hands over his body, found nothing, and announced "I can't find any leaks"55

"You son of a bitch," Shepherd responded, "That scared the shit out of me".56

Simmons went below, looking for a cup of coffee and a cigarette. His head ached. When he removed his helmet

---

54 Hell on Keels 2877
55 ibid
56 ibid

he found a chunk of shrapnel almost an inch long had been caught by his helmet. It had saved his life. All he had was a severe headache from a concussion, and his ear was bleeding.

 Enemy fire was bursting around the boat as the TiCL4 smoke began to make a curtain. John Ladd quickly turned his boat 90 degrees away from where the smoke screen had been laid. Japanese gunfire continued to be aimed into the smoke as PT-151 pulled away. The Japanese kept on firing for about 16 minutes. Enemy fire was fairly accurate and PT-151 took a number of shrapnel hits in the dayroom, transom, and rocket rack. One muffler rod was severed and the cable holding one depth charge was nearly cut. The steel helmets that all the crew wore proved their value. Five of them were creased by shrapnel but the men wearing them were unharmed. While this was going on there was another crisis in PT-151. The port engine died. There were 3-4 anxious minutes until MoMM3c Robert Smith aided by MoMM2c Norman Philip Thomas in the engine room brought it back on line. While they worked, the depth charges that were in place of the other torpedoes were released in the hope that the plumes of water they tossed up when detonating would confuse the Japanese gunners. The speed of PT-151 on only 2 engines was just 15 knots. During all this her radio operator, RM3c John

Patrick Frayne, was continuously trying to get out a contact report. Despite his efforts, there was no acknowledgement. Not only was contact lost up the chain of command, but there was now also no radio communication with the other boats of the section.

PT-151 headed for the sections' prearranged rendezvous point on the eastern side of Limasawa. ENS Boo Grosscup's PT-146 had arrived there about 30 minutes earlier, and was briefly illuminated by Japanese star shells. The enemy fired 4 rounds of larger caliber, probably 4.7", at PT-146. The projectiles landed some 300 yards away. The Japanese ship then broke off the action. The two Elco boats continued to search for PT-190, but they were not successful. About 0330 the radioman on PT-151 heard PT-190 sending a contact report to the squadron tender, USS WACHAPREAGUE. The section commander now knew all his boats had survived the hail of Japanese gunfire, but he was still unable to contact PT-190. At 0535 he received a distress call from PT-194 and took his 2 boats toward Sonok Point on Panaon Island in order to render aid, if necessary. At 0610 they joined PT-194 and PT-196. The four boats began the return trip to their home tender. En route they were joined by PT-152 and PT-190.

PT-190 Edward Stanley Haugen as CDR in 1963-
fold3.com

PT-190   Navsource 120319001

Left PT-146 TM2c Clifford Edward Cook obit photo
ancestry.com

13 SW Panaon PTs PT-150, PT-194, PT-196

LT Roman George Mislicky, age 30, the executive officer of MTBRON 12, was in command of the section assigned to patrol around the southern tip of Panoan Island. Mislicky started his military career as a 16 year old in 1930 when he attended an Army run Civilian Military Training Camp in Illinois. He enlisted in the navy in 1932 and was selected for training as an officer when the US joined the war. He was commissioned in June, 1942. His temporary promotion to LT was dated from July 1944. Not surprisingly, he was known as 'Slick' in the squadron. He rode in PT-196 which was commanded by LTJG James R. Beck from Birmingham AL. The other boats in his section were PT-194 and PT-150.

At the time, PT-196 was named 'Purple Shaft', and she carried a large white star on the forward deck for aircraft recognition. Her armament had also undergone a few changes. The positions of the forward 37mm and 20mm guns had been swapped and she carried 2 additional twin 0.50 Cal. machineguns just forward of the cockpit, one on each side.

LT Roman George Mislicky   Obituary photo from ancestry.com

PT-196 LTJG James Richard Beck – ancestry.com

Into the Jaws of Death

 PT-194 was commanded by 5' 11" LTJG Thomas C. Hall from Denton, TX; and PT-150 by 23 year old LTJG William J. West.

MTBRON 12 boats were painted navy dark blue over all, with grey numbers outlined in white on both sides of the bridge.

PT-196 astern of WACHAPREAGUE   80-G-345815

PT 196 officers in New Guinea- from ptboatforum.com

F1c Fred Adler from PT-196 would later comment about their assignment, "Our job was to be a decoy for the destroyers. Why would you risk a destroyer when you could risk a PT boat which isn't worth $1,000?57".

The 3 boat section shoved off from tender WACHAPREAGUE in Liloan Bay at 1830. When they reached their assigned area off the southern tip of Panoan Island, about 30 minutes later, they lay to and began searching both with radar and visually. All 3 boats used their engines intermittently to remain on station and counter the effects of tides and currents. On PT-196 both the radio and radar were not performing well with

---

[57] Hell on Keels 2793

the later indicating many false targets. Finally, at 0300, the radar on PT-196 failed completely. LT Mislicky did not want to operate without radar and therefore transferred to PT-194.

At about 2000 the weather had begun to deteriorate. Clouds and rain limited visibility. This would continue throughout the entire night. At 0445 the glow of a fire was seen to the northeast. It was not readily apparent just how far away it was. The boats moved a bit further into the strait to help make a better identification. On PT-194 the radar was noted to be "hot and sweating ". Of course, PT-196 had no functioning radar at all. By 0500 the radar on PT-150 had 2 targets at 6000 yards that appeared to be moving southwest at high speed. The first view from PT-194 was that they might be other MTBs from another patrol sector. Within 5 minutes they could be tentatively identified as Japanese destroyers. Another 2 minutes and the targets removed any doubts by opening fire on the three PTs.

The three boats came right and began travelling on almost a parallel track. On the bridge of 'Purple Shaft' skipper Tommy Hall shouted "Smoke! Give me smoke!"[58]

---

[58] Hell on Keels

The Titanium tetrachloride smoke generators were opened to make life more difficult for the Japanese optical directors that would be searching for them. For the next 30 minutes the exchange of fire continued. PT-150 fired one torpedo and expended some 20mm and 37mm rounds from her forward guns before turning sharply toward Balongbalong and setting the throttles of all three engines to maximum speed. This maneuver caused her to lose contact with the other 2 boats by 0520.

The Japanese concentrated their fire on PT-194, and their shooting was accurate. TM3c Wilbur Allen Smith from Lincoln, IL, along with TM3c Andrew Gavel set their torpedo to run at a depth of 30 feet. But when they launched it, it just sank, harmlessly, into the depths. Japanese fire was too hot, and the distance too great, to attempt another torpedo shot. The first enemy salvo had put the 40mm gun on PT-194's fantail out of service after it had fired only one round. The 37mm bow gun was disabled before it ever had a chance to shoot back. The left gun in the starboard twin 0.50 turret was also disabled. One 4.7" Japanese shell struck the boat aft, tearing a hole in the lazarette below the water line. The water tight bulkhead to the engine room was peppered with holes. And the resultant flooding caused the boat to lose both trim and speed. An enemy 40mm round scored a hit on the cockpit about 5 minutes after the boat had turned away. It seriously wounded the leg of the radioman, 18 year old Alfred Arthur Messier from Hartford, Conn. Shrapnel from this same round hit the right leg of LT Mislicky, and flying debris struck him in the head and knocked him, senseless, to the deck. Mislicky remained unconscious for about 10 minutes. Shrapnel also made holes in the starboard exhaust vent of the port engine.

Brown eyed TM3c Andrew ('Andy') Gavel, one of 194's torpedo men, was standing near the cockpit on the boat's port side. He described the next events like this: "We made a run and I just managed to drop a torpedo over the port side. The guys on the thirty-seven-millimeter were firing on one of the Japanese ships. Then, as we swerved, the star shells lit us up like daylight. Next thing I knew they got us with a five-incher in the stern. Harold Jenkins[59], the pointer on the aft forty-millimeter, got hit. He was a cop from Philly, the oldest guy on the boat, thirty-six, I think. The shell also knocked out two of our engines, so we only had one left. We began putting out smoke. It seemed like they were peppering us with everything; quite a few people

---

[59] The name Harold Jenkins doesn't appear in either the Action reports or the muster rolls

got shrapnel, but not me. With only one engine, we just had to wait it out. We couldn't do anything more."60

One of those Japanese shells made a hole in the dayroom canopy as it entered. It also set off spare 20mm ammunition and shell fragments cut the control line to the CO_2 fire smothering system in the engine room. The resultant release of CO_2 killed the engines and left the boat without power. Another hit started a fire in the officer's quarters. On deck, TM2c Harry Robert Carlson from Denver, Colorado, received multiple shrapnel injuries on his back. The other two officers in the cockpit suffered minor shrapnel injuries that did not incapacitate them. LTJG Thomas C. Hall continued to direct, and inspire, his crew. His direction helped the badly battered boat to survive. His second officer, 6' 3" ENS James Manning Bruett, had been a star player and captain of the school's 1938 football team at Syracuse University. Now, he operated the TICL4 smoke generator to confuse the Japanese gunners and then later turned his attention to treating other injured crew members.

Nearby, PT-195 could see the Japanese fire hitting all around PT-194. The Skipper, ENS William Diver, turned

---

[60] Voices p108

to his passenger/observer LTJG Leo Henry Leary and remarked, "God Almighty, Slick's getting it."[61]

Possibly the most important actions that resulted in the survival of PT-194 were those of the men in the engine room. The Japanese shell that injured LT Mislicky had also activated the CO_2 smothering system designed to prevent an engine room fire. All three Packard motors were temporarily silenced. The engine room crew opened exhaust vents to air out the space. 26 year old MoMM2c Earl Roy Welker, who had married his sweetheart, Gladys, in 1937, took the lead. The former Idaho resident would do things to make sure he could return to her. He restarted the engines and restored power to the badly battered boat. Alongside him was MoMM2c John Ora Bozman from Ohio. Bozman worked tirelessly to assist with restarting the engines and to control the flooding coming from the holes in the bulkhead to the lazarette.

---

[61] Wooden boats at war

PT 194 MoMM2c John O. Bozman and wife

Despite his shattered leg, Radioman Messier managed to get out a call for help to the other boats. And other boats responded. PT-196 located PT-194, came alongside, and transferred a pharmacist's mate and two other men to aid in handling injuries and bringing the boat home. Messier then turned the radio over to S1c Charles Stephen Kuehn. Teen aged Arnold Estep from Ohio, the boats' cook, also helped tend the injured. He applied a bandage to Frank Adler's injured arm, and then went through the medicine cabinets where he found a packet of sulfanilamide powder. He poured the contents onto Alfred Messier's shattered leg.

It seems the Japanese really had been listening to the American radio frequencies. The following excerpt from Hell on Keels would certainly support the idea.

The RM on PT-194 was surprised to hear a clear request, in English, as the boat was trying to evade enemy gunfire.

"Who's the skipper of the 194 boat?"

"Mr. Hall." Responded S1c (RM) Charles Kuhn, who had taken over when Messier was wounded.

"Mr. Hall will be in hell tonight", the unknown voice continued, "And will never sail against the Japanese Imperial Fleet again".

The answer came from ENS John Ladd in PT-151 in a nearby patrol area, "Don't worry about those dirty Jap SOBs, Tommy, we're coming to help you".62

Alabama born James Richard Beck's PT-196 was the first to reach the damaged PT-194. His torpedoman, 5' 10" TM3c Charles Norman Kantner Jr., jumped across to the stricken Liberty Hound and immediately began using a bucket to bail out water from the partly flooded compartments of the damaged PT boat.

---

[62] Hell on Keels

Chaos reigned in the engine room of PT-194. All three Packard engines were temporarily dead. F1c Fred Adler had been alone in the space when the Japanese shell struck. His right arm was injured and bleeding. He threw open the hatches and intakes to clear out the CO2 that had smothered the engines, and then, using only his left arm, restarted the first one and its' associated electric generator. He was screaming for help while doing this. MoMM2c Earl Roy Welker and MoMM1c John Ora Bozman came to assist. The two men restarted the other engines and Bozman went to work trying to plug the shrapnel holes in the bulkhead to the lazarette from which a steady stream of sea water was threatening to flood the engine room. With power restored, PT-194 limped away to lick her wounds.

PT-150 had become separated from the others. She heard, and logged, the call from PT-194. Being without radar, she was unable to contribute much. By 0630 she was heading toward San Ricardo Point and shortly after that sighted an enemy cruiser, probably on fire and trailing smoke, retiring from the area. This contact was promptly reported. The boat had not forgotten that their primary duty was to detect and report Japanese movements. At 0705 PT-150, then all alone, called for permission to return to base. The request was granted.

PT 150 LT William West Jr. Navsource 120515010

PT 150 TM Wilfred Langdon Wooddell Navsource
120515011

PT 150 S1c Walter Joseph Flynn Providence RI
Navsource 120515012

PT 150 Wendell Floyd ('Skip') Inskeep cook Navsource
120515006

PT 150 GM Rudolph Charles ('Andy') Gesik Navsource 120515008

PT-150 QM William Ernest Garfield Navsource 120515013

PT 150 Bob Weise, LTJG Smiles, Bob Machnik, LT West-
Navsource 120515009

TM Robert Paul Weise and LTJG William Jeffrey Smiles
were involved in the fight. S2c Robert Machnik joined
the crew after the Surigao battle. The 7 photographs
above come from Navsource and appear on that site in
color. They come from the collection of Bob Machnik
and were donated by Jerry Gilmartin.

PT-196 GM3c William Thomas Detherage
ancestry.com

PT-196 TM3c Charles Norman Kantner Jr. ancestry.com

PT-194 ENS James Bruett Syracuse tackle and captain 1939 yearbook

PT-194 GM3c Hugo Aloysius Hanke 1942 HS photo ancestry.com

A day later all PT operations were suspended as a typhoon, wryly designated Tropical Depression Eighteen passed over the area. The boats moved away from the tenders to avoid being pounded to pieces against the side of their mother ships by the winds. Four boats, including PT-194, were driven aground. The Executive Officer, ENS Bruett, managed to restart one of the

Packard engines and the 'Liberty Hound' was gently moved back out to the bay with almost no damage.

A Japanese air raid came after some boats a few days later. Two single engine aircraft attacked PT-196. TM2c Charles Francis Denison on the 37mm gun forward downed the first one with only a few rounds. The gun crew on the after 40mm took out the second raider. The crew members involved were; 20 year old New Jersey native GM3c Hugo Aloysius Hanke, the pointer, S1c Junius Paul ('Frenchy') Duplantis from Louisiana, the trainer, brown eyed 18 year old SC3c Harold Richard Jero, first loader, and S1c Robert Anderson from Connecticut, second loader.63

____

[63] The Portsmouth Star Sunday December 10th, 1944

14 Madilao Point PTs PT-195, PT-191, PT-192

Section 5 was commanded by LCDR Theodore Roosevelt Stansbury riding in PT-192 Stansbury had an unusual background as a member of the PT fraternity. He was 40 years old and had attended the Naval Academy in Annapolis from 1923 to 1927, where he lettered in football and boxing. The other midshipmen called him 'Cowboy'. He was commissioned as an Ensign and served in the battleship USS WEST VIRGINIA. He resigned his commission in October, 1929 and became a civilian. He was working for the Pabst Brewing Company in sales in New York when the Japanese attacked Pearl Harbor. He returned to serve in the navy and his previous service was taken into account. At the time of the action he was a LCDR, and still spoke with the South Kentucky accent that he had from before his time at Annapolis.

PT-191 LCDR Theodore Roosevelt Stansbury – USNA
Lucky Bag 1927

ENS Ted R Stansbury in 1928 from ancestry.com
Beautylynch73600

PT-191 carried 2 twin machine gun mounts on the deck, just forward of the pilot house. Prior to departure the men disassembled and cleaned all the guns, with particular attention to eliminating any signs of rust. Rust forms in the presence of water, and there was LOTS of rain in the Philippines at this time of the year. Afterwards the weapons were put back together and tested. Fuel tanks were topped off. Helmets and kapok life jackets were stowed on the outside of the day room. Crew members took their helmets and donned long trousers and long sleeved shirts before sortieing. Doing this was mandatory on patrol as leg protection was important to avoid flash burns from enemy fire and also because when firing the guns the ejected spent shell casings were very hot. QM3c Joseph Nash Myers cleaned the starboard 0.50 machine gun he manned. Myers, a 23 year old from Pennsylvania, had been part of the crew since the end of July. But he already had garnered some experiences that few others had. In May, while en route to join MTB Squadron 12, Joe Myers had crossed the equator at sea and became a shellback. He kept the certificate shown below. Later, in January, 1945, his boat was attacked by a Japanese plane. The bomb that was dropped missed the boat by a short distance, and Joe kept shooting at it even though he was wounded. That earned him both a Purple Heart medal and a Silver Star, America's third highest award for heroism. That attack also killed one of his shipmates, MoMM2c Robert William ('Bob') Rauch, and wounded another, S1c (GM) Ed Morris Galimore.

There are some interesting items relating to Ed Galimore. He was born in rural North Carolina and the first time he appeared in the US census, in 1930, the census taker listed him as a girl named Edna. The next census, in 1940, corrected the gender, but listed his name as "Ednie". He joined MTBRON 12 in July, 1944, along with Joe Myers. His statement about being wounded is included below.

PT-195   navsource 120519501600

PT-191 GM3c Ed Morris Galimore ancestry.com

PT-192 LTJG Kester Denman 1937 at Stephen F. Austin
Univ. ancestry.com

To whom it may concern:
This is the patrol when I was wounded. I had seen worst times before. It was about midnight on January 25, 1945. We were patrolling near Cebu Island in the Philippines. The patrol was almost over and we were getting ready to head back home. A Japanese plane came over a mountaintop and started a bomb attack on us. The bomb exploded about 5 feet from the stern of the boat. The boat was completely covered with flames from the blast. A piece of the shrapnel went through the collar of my life jacket at the back of my neck. Another piece hit me in the left arm. Over one half of the crew was wounded. Myers was seriously wounded. I never saw him again but heard he recovered. Bob Rauch was killed. He was hit in the head with shrapnel. A few more feet and he would have been safe inside the hatch. He was near me when he got hit. His blood ran under my feet. He gave me a rain coat just a day or two before he was killed. I had been on worse patrols with more wounded. The worse thing I saw was a direct hit on a P.T. boat by a bomb from a Japanese plane. There was nothing left but a little of the forepeak .There were no survivors. This was during the Invasion of the Philippines at Layte Island. If you went 10 minutes without shooting at a plane you were doing good.

Ed M. Galimore

PT-191 statement from Ed Galimore, used with permission from Deborah ancestry.com

ENS William Diver commanded PT-195, named 'Toodles". She carried an extra observer from the squadron staff, LT Leo Henry Leary. Leary had been sent to Communications School before heading to the Pacific. He was heir to a large fortune and was one of a group of officers assigned to MTBRON 12 that had resulted in the unit being informally called the millionaires' squadron. The Vanderbilt brothers, Alfred and George, were also part of that group, but had reached the fighting earlier. Alfred had already been rotated back to the USA before the voyage to Leyte, and his brother, George, the squadron intelligence officer, followed soon after.

The 3 PTs; 191,192, and 195, left for their assigned station at 1815. An hour and a half later they were off the West coast of Mindanao. All three boats stayed together. This did limit the area that could be observed visually, but really made little difference. This section made no direct contacts. PT-191, skippered by LTJG Nelson ('Nels') Davis, couldn't even detect the enemy by radar because her SO radar set was not operational throughout the entire battle. Nels had been on the swimming team at the University of Michigan before joining the Navy. The section was stationed in an area that was the farthest to the south, and not in line with the path of the advancing Japanese. The boats remained together either lying to or maneuvering at very slow speed to remain on station. Consequently they also did not engage any Japanese ships. They were not directly involved in combat.

But that did not mean they were completely out of the action. They heard reports on the radio and saw the flashes of gunfire and the bursting star shells. ENS Diver observed the Japanese shooting at PTs in a nearby section and remarked to Leo Leary "God Almighty, Slick's getting it".[64] It was true. LT Mislicky's section was engaged in a serious firefight as reported in Chapter 13. But seeing flashes in the distance was as close as this trio of boats would get to actual combat that night.

---

[64] Hell on Keels 2942

PT 191 QM2c Joseph Nash Myers fold3.com

PT 191 MoMM2c Robert William Rauch findagrave.com

PT-192 had a pair of men that had trained as torpedo men; Kenneth Duane Christianson, and Macon Lavern

Stinnette. The other crew members called them, probably predictably, Criss and Mac. Mac Stinnette, from Bossier, LA., spent his first tour of active duty on a North Atlantic escort; the old destroyer, USS DECATUR (DD-341). It seems he got tired of the cold and decided to volunteer for PT duty in order to get to the warmer climes of the South Pacific. He reported to MTBRON12 in September, 1944. Christianson, from South Dakota, was six feet tall and blue eyed, and had joined the squadron just a little more than a week earlier. Their torpedo expertise was not used during the Surigao battle.

Right PT-192 TM2c Macon ('Mac') Lavern Stinnette
ancestry.co

Left PT-191 officers –skipper Nels Davis on right
ptboatforum.com

Right PT-195 LTJG Leo Henry Leary HS photo
ancestry.com

PT-191 did get to play a positive role, even though her radar was not working. Skipper Nels Davis was the first boat to come to the rescue of badly damaged   PT-194.

The forward mounted 37mm on PT-195 was under the control of TM2c Charles Francis Denison from Buffalo, NY. He would normally have been assigned to a torpedo launching rack, but he had shown that he was an expert marksman by picking off tin cans in the water with one of the older Springfield bolt action rifles. The bow gun was often the first weapon to engage the enemy in a gun fight. He had even tried to volunteer to go as the gunner on LTJG Joe Eddins' PT-152 before learning that his own PT-195 was also going out.65

PT-195 ENS William Stowell Diver college photo 1938

---

[65] Hell on Keels

PT 191 refueling en route to Leyte-Navsource
120519101

PT -195 and crew   ptforum.photogallery.image.jjGrt

PT195 MoMM2c Jerry Jerome Donovan   ancestry.com

PT-192 TM1c Kenneth Duane Christianson {arrow}
ancestry.com

15 SE Panaon PTs PT-134, PT-132, PT-137

LCDR Robert Leeson, the commander of MTBRON 7 and who had led the boats on their epic journey from New Guinea, commanded the section assigned to the southwest of Panoan Island. He rode in PT-134, commanded by Edmund F Wakelin from Holyoke, MA. The section arrived on station at 1910.All three boats were about 200 yards off Binit Point and within visual range of each other

PT-132 Navsource 120513201

PT-134 bridge Navsource 120513402

At 2300 Leeson received the first enemy contact report made by PT-127. Only 15 minutes later PT-134's radar picked up an approaching target. As PT-134, named 'Eight Ball', tracked the advancing Japanese he sent out a stream of contact reports. They were relayed via LT Orrell's PT-523 in an adjacent patrol area because Leeson's own boat was unable to communicate directly.

PT-134 RM3c Lester V. Chalmers Jr. findagrave.com

LCDR Robert Leeson The Boston Globe Fri Oct 27 1944

PT-134 LTJG Ed Wakelin   Holyoke Telegram 7 Nov 1944 p 1

The log entries from earlier in the night indicate that the crew was awake and alert:

"   2135 aircraft on course NE. 134 was lying to off Binit Village. a/c was 150 true at 4 miles, heading 045.

        2235 2 planes headed N. bearing 090 range 3 miles.

        0045 star shell 10 miles south of the tip of Panoan. Might have come from an aircraft.

        0115 unidentified radar contact bearing 235 range 8 miles from southern tip of Panoan. Targets plotted as zig zagging."

At 0130 Wakelin's boat got underway from where she had been waiting. All 3 Packard engines were running, mufflers closed. The boats headed off on course 055, speed 10 knots. The intention was to get closer to the radar contacts. Their primary mission of reporting the advancing Japanese had been fulfilled. Now it was time to think about attacking. Speed was soon increased to 15 knots. The other two boats were ordered to follow in order to achieve a favorable firing position. Communications with the other two boats of the section was lost shortly after that order was given. PTs 132 and 137 became separated and made their attacks independently. By 0150 PT-134's target resolved into 2 large ships screened by three smaller vessels ahead. The targets were 2 miles off the starboard beam.

PT-134's second officer, 20 year old ENS Howard Irwin Green from NY, was in the cockpit as the boat came right to intercept the center of the enemy formation with a more favorable position for launching torpedoes at the bigger targets. At 0205, when 3000 yards from the enemy, one of the Japanese switched on a searchlight and caught 'Eight Ball' directly in the beam. Every gun that could be aimed at the searchlights began firing. ENS Green later said "We kept right on into those searchlights at top speed until we were 1500 yards from the battleship. Then we let go three torpedoes, swerving away from the light. We don't know what we hit, but we heard a loud explosion and our boat shuddered from the concussion."66

RM3c Lester Vermont Chalmers, a six foot tall 20 year old from Raleigh, NC, was near ENS Green in the cockpit. He confirmed what Green saw. "It was shot out immediately" said Chalmers, regarding the searchlight.

The heavy torpedo tubes and the not too reliable Mark VIII torpedoes they originally carried had been replaced by the newer Mark XIII that rested in a two part light weight cradle attached to the PTs deck. The torpedo was held in place by a two piece cable that was wrapped around the body of the torpedo and joined in a single release hook located between the cradle parts. When ordered to launch, the crewman stationed at the torpedo released the holding cable and raised the lever arms on the cradle parts. The torpedo simply rolled over the side. As it fell, another light cable was pulled out of the body of the torpedo and started the torpedo motor. Depth and direction settings were pre-set, so the weapon able to proceed independently after launch. The reason only three of PT-134's torpedoes were fired

---

66 NY Daily news 4 Nov 1944

was that the crew member on the fourth 'fish' did not hear the order to launch.

PT-134 MoMM3c Pat John D'Amico   NY Daily News 3 Nov 1944

PT-134 ENS Howard Irwin Green   Sideboy p62

The Japanese ships had opened fire and bracketed PT-134 on all sides, and with air bursts overhead. PT-134 replied with all guns. She had launched 3 torpedoes before coming hard right to retire on course 260 at full speed. The searchlight followed 134 for only a few minutes before shifting to other targets, but it returned later. All 3 boats of the section were making separate attacks, and all were active. After the action it was determined that PT-134 had expended 24 rounds of 40mm, 30 rounds of 37mm, 120 rounds of 20mm and 500 rounds of 0.50 cal. when firing at Japanese searchlights.

ENS Green added "We didn't stand around to watch because it was the first time a PT took on a whole enemy task force and we wanted to live to tell the story."67

After 0230 the radio circuit was overloaded and attempts to contact any other units were extremely difficult to impossible. By 0250 PT-134 was again lying to off Binit Village when the next group of 4 Japanese destroyers was detected. Her last torpedo was launched, aimed at the lead destroyer. MoMM3c Pat D'Amico from the Bronx thought they had scored a hit, but the torpedo was seen to miss astern.

There were more contacts later, but since PT-134 had no more torpedoes, they were not pursued.

---

[67] The Spokane WA Spokesman-Review Fri Nov 3 1944

Boston Globe reporter Martin Sheridan was on board PT-132. He was the only war correspondent on any of the PT boats that night. He filed his stories with the North American Newspaper Alliance, a syndicate that provided pooled reports from overseas correspondents to dozens of papers all across America. The skipper of PT-132, ENS Paul Henry Jones from Indianapolis, had spoken to him as the boats cast off for their mission

"We've always had action with correspondents aboard," He said then, "I hope I don't disappoint you."68

At about 0220 PT-132, named 'Sea Bat', made contact with a Japanese destroyer about a mile south of Binit Point. War correspondent Martin Sheridan had been dozing on the top of the desk house and was wakened by a call by ENS Jones, "There they are, dead ahead, just rounding the tip of the island"69

The skipper of PT-132 maneuvered the boat to launch an attack. Her torpedo men; Albert Aime Berard, a five foot three inch former jockey who was nicknamed 'Sharkey', five foot ten Wilburn Lee Burnett, and William James Speer from San Francisco, were all standing by their racks. So was TM3c Joe Gigac who

---

68 Sheridan – Scranton PA Times-Tribune 25 Nov 1944 p4
69 Sheridan – Scranton PA Times-Tribune 25 Nov 1944 p4

belonged to PT-523 of MTBRON36 but had been loaned to PT-132 when it looked like his own boat would not be ready on time. Second officer, ENS Robert Harold Muller Jr, computed the torpedo settings.

Watching over the 3 Packard engines was MoMM1c Edwin Sherburn Bowers from Oregon. He was nicknamed 'Whitie' because of his light complexion and blond hair. Eighteen year old Jimmie Dale Hopkins was the youngest engine room team member. He had reported to the squadron on June first.

PT-132 Edwin Sherwin Bowers   findagrave.com

PT-132 James Dale Hopkins   Young American Patriots

The first torpedo rolled off with a splash and headed towards the target, but missed by a few yards.

"Fire two" Jones yelled, followed by "Fire three".70

He fired all 4 of his mark XIII torpedoes, one by one, at about 1200 yards. All missed. The last one actually malfunctioned and headed away from the target. The boat turned away, but then reversed with the thought of trying to get within rocket range. It wasn't a good idea, and was swiftly discarded. PT-132 withdrew. She was not fired on. Contact with the enemy was lost and 132 returned to a position between Binit and Bolobolo village where she remained, close to shore to avoid detection. She made no further attacks as all her torpedoes had been expended.

---

70 ibid

PT-137, named 'The Duchess' had problems with her radio and radar throughout the night. The radar was totally out of service all night, and her VHF transmitter also. Her auxiliary generator was not functioning and storage batteries were low.

ENS Paul Henry Jones   ancestry.com

LCDR Isadore Martin Kovar   Kittanning PA Leader-Times
1 nov-1957

At 0125, when she lost sight of PT-134, 'The Duchess' returned to her original patrol station. At 0215 made visual contact with passing enemy destroyers. The enemy was almost on top of them. The boat got underway and managed to launch one torpedo, which missed, at the trailing enemy ship. PT-134 then retired undetected.

At 0305 heavy firing was observed north of Panoan. PT-137 moved out into Surigao strait and at 0335 made visual contact with a Japanese destroyer that was heading south. LTJG Isadore Martin Kovar, commanding PT-137, closed and launched her port aft torpedo. An explosion was heard about 30 seconds later and the enemy commenced firing star shells. Kovar's boat remained undetected during this attack although star shells were overhead from about 0320 to 0520. The torpedo was set to run at a depth of 10 feet and passed right under the intended target. As it continued, it struck the Japanese light cruiser ABUKUMA just below the bridge. The cruiser was disabled. She did manage to stay afloat, only to be polished off by US aircraft the next day.

LTJG Kovar received the Navy Cross for sinking the Japanese cruiser that was not his original target. Mike

Kovar had married before being sent to the South Pacific. He paid $0.50 for the marriage license.

PT-137 picked up a radio distress call from PT-194 at 0510 and headed to assist. The trip was interrupted by enemy destroyer that fired at PT-137 at about 0534. 'The Duchess' fell into company with PT-150 and both boats searched, unsuccessfully, for PT-194 before returning to the tenders.

PT-132 S1c Dumont A. Souleyrette Navsource 120513202.

PT-132 QM2c Herbert Henry Betz The Liberal News 09 Jul 1948 page 1 Betz died aboard USS COMFORT (AH-3) and was initially buried in the Philippines. This photo is from when his body was returned to the US for reburial.

The three PTs of Bob Leeson's section all made it home from the battle that night. But the war was not over. On th2 night of 26-27 October PT-132 was out again. This time she was paired with PT-326 from MTBRON12 for a mission involving delivering some special Army forces from a unit called the Alamo Scouts. The major part of the job went off smoothly, but not the trip home. A Japanese fighter plane spotted them and dove in to make a bombing run. The two PT boats zigzagged and the gunners threw up a curtain of anti-aircraft fire. RM3c Kenton Thomas Gibson was at the helm of the Sea Bat. His maneuvers kept the boat from harm, but not all the crew. The single bomb that was dropped landed about 30 yards behind PT-132. The fragments struck most of the men who were topside. TM2c William James Speer was killed outright. Fragments from the bomb penetrated the kapok lifejackets of others. The wounded included the skipper, ENS Paul Henry Jones, and his XO, ENS Bob Muller. Other crew members that had survived the fighting in Surigao but not this bomb included; MoMM1c Whitie Bowers, MoMM1c Robert John Parazinski, MoMM3c Jimmie Dale Hopkins, and QM2c Herbert Henry Betz. Betz died from his wounds two days later.

PT-132 TM2c William James Speer – ancestry.com

PT-132 RM3c Owen Milton Beach - 0bit photo
ancestry.com

16 Bilaa Point PTs PT-494, PT-497, PT-324

The section assigned to patrol off Bilaa Point was made up from boats that belonged to different squadrons. The section commander, New York born LT Joseph H Moran II, was also commander of PT-494. Squadron mate PT-497 under LTJG Joseph Carl Beckman Jr. from Tacoma, Washington was the second boat. Both were part of MTBRON33. The third boat, PT-324, came from MTBRON21. Six foot 2 inch tall ENS Harrell Fisher Dumas was her commander. The mixing of vessels from separate squadrons meant that the boats and crews had less experience working together. It was caused by having a number of PTs being repaired after the long ride from New Guinea when the original patrol sections were set up. Before the boats actually departed a number of those being worked on were declared ready for duty and were assigned to sections that had originally been only two PTs.

PT-494   Navsource 120549401

The boats left for patrol at 1520, local time. Sunset was at 1818, local time. They cruised at an economical speed in order to save fuel and were on station at 1945. The moon had already gone down and it was a dark night. The three boats had been out for nearly 6 hours when they got their first radar contact on ships moving north into the strait at 0110. There was no visual contact. The enemy was tracked as proceeding at 25 knots. They passed PT-497 at a range of about 9 miles. About an hour later large caliber gunfire was heard and a fire was seen about 8 miles west of Kantahid Point. Radar soon showed a target approaching the patrol area. PT-497 remained in place while observing the enemy firing at another PT section. Skipper Beckman wanted to attack, but in the absence of a command from his section leader, he continued to just lie to and observe.

PT-497 Joseph Carl Beckman 1938   HS graduation picture ancestry.com

PT-497 Herbert Haile Chace San Diego State yearbook 1940

PT-494 Joseph H. Moran ------eating on the bridge

Tugboat named Joseph H. Moran ii

The officer in tactical command was LT Joseph H. Moran in PT-494. Mike Moran was no stranger to the sea. His grandfather founded Moran Tugs and Towing, NYCs largest tugboat operator. He Himself qualified as a tugboat seaman in 1932, and even had a Moran company tugboat named after him. Mike felt the enemy targets that they saw were outside his section's patrol area, and when first detected, had already passed his patrol line. Chasing them would have left his patrol area unguarded against possible enemy vessels escaping through his area. His section stayed where it was.

PT-324 was a dutiful subordinate. The boats held their position and missed out on a more direct contribution to the fight. At 0545 the squadron commander ordered them by radio to head for Sumilon Island. They joined PT-523, 524, and 526 at around 0630. Together, the boats began the slow cruise back to their tender, USS WACHAPREAGUE.

PT-497   Navsource 120549701

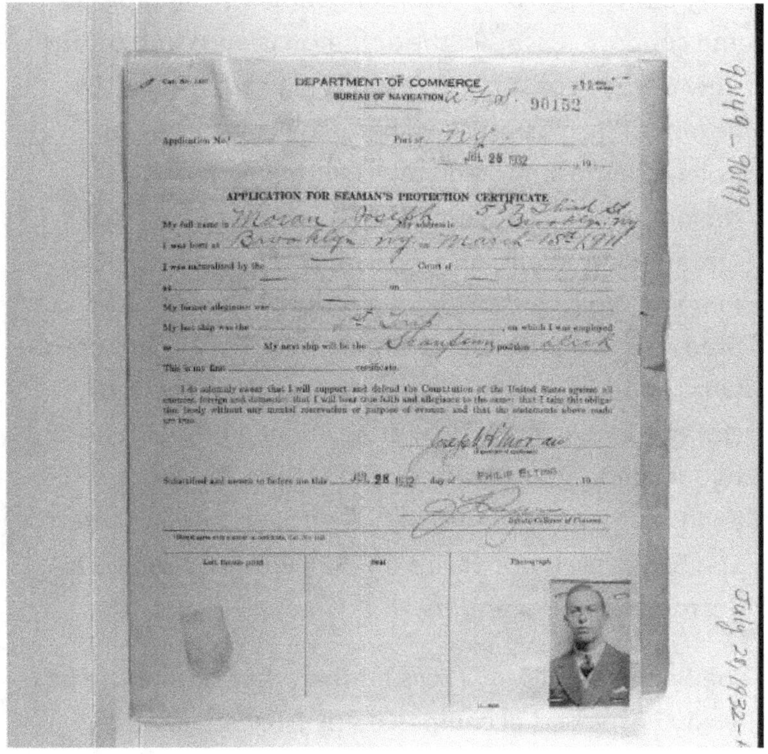

PT-494 Joseph Moran - seaman certificate 1932

The boats in this section didn't take an active part in the fighting that night, but they would get a chance to make up for it in a very short time. With the defeat of the Japanese navy in the straights the focus on their side shifted to reinforcing the army units on Leyte Island.

This was a scenario the PT squadrons knew well. PT boat patrols had been attacking Japanese landing craft and support vessels in the Solomon Islands and off the New Guinea coast for the past two years. The MTBs began offensive patrols to keep the Leyte garrison isolated almost immediately. On the night of 9-10 November 4 boats were covering Ormoc Bay in pairs. LT Alexander W Wells with PT-524, skippered by LTJG James P Wolf,-and PT-525 under ENS Gervis Stuart Brady was on one side of Ormoc Bay. They encountered what appeared to be a Japanese supply vessel and closed to investigate. Just after midnight PT-525 fired two torpedoes at it, but missed. At the same time PT-524 fired two torpedoes at a destroyer, missing astern. The 525 retired under fire. PT-524 was pursued by a destroyer for 45 minutes.[71]

Joe Beckman's PT-497 was on the other side of the bay. Many Pesos was accompanied by PT-492, named 'Impatient Virgin', under the command of LT Mel Haines. Squadron 33 commander, LCDR Arthur Murray Preston, was in overall command. They encountered a trio of Japanese destroyers. Beckman, who had been captain of his Washington State football team, did not

---

[71] Bulkeley At Close Quarters p 395

hesitate. He headed toward the Japanese and alerted his crew.

"Stand by your fish".

The Japanese destroyers were about 1800 yards away when the PTs launched their mark XIII torpedoes. Joe Beckman gave the orders in sequence.

"Fire One."

"Fire Two."

"Fire Three."

"Fire Four".

At each command one of the men standing by the torpedo cradle pulled the safety pin and lifted the handles. The torpedo rolled off the side of the boat. The umbilical cord attached to it pulled free and the torpedo motor started. The 'fish' began its' run toward the enemy. With the last torpedo launched the second officer, ENS Herbert Haile Chace, spun the wheel quickly and the boat swung sharply away and began to withdraw at full speed. At the same time the enemy destroyers turned on their searchlights and pointed them towards the attackers. PT-492 also launched 4 torpedoes before the illumination began. She, too, turned rapidly to withdraw. Both boats activated the TCl4 cylinders astern and laid a thick cloud of chemical smoke behind them as they crisscrossed each other's wakes. This is how the event was recorded in Joe Myers diary as related by the radioman "The 492 fired all 4 of her fish and missed. Our skipper gave the order 'stand by torpedoes'. We slipped in closer till we were only 1500 yards away. Then the order 'Fire!' My heart was beating like a trip hammer. 2 minutes later there was a terrific explosion and a blinding flash of orange light. Red hot pieces of metal flew all over the bay. Everyone started cheering 'we hit her!' Then a searchlight from one of the 2 remaining cans turned on the 492. She was lit up plain as day. A couple of seconds later the other can put her searchlight on us. We both opened our engines wide and started speeding the hell out of there. The 2 cans started firing salvos of 5 inchers at us. Shells were falling all around us thick and heavy. I was expecting one to hit us any minute. We turned on our smoke bottle. For exactly 18 minutes the cans kept chasing us and gaining. Then we cut between 2 small islands and the cans stopped chasing and firing at us. The must have thought we were leading them into a trap. We headed back to the base safe and sound with a Jap destroyer to our credit"

The destroyers chased the boats down the edge of Ponson Island, only giving up the pursuit when the PT's passed through narrow Kawit Strait between Ponson and Poro islands. The Japanese gunfire failed to score any hits. But the torpedoes did. One target disappeared from the radar and LCDR Preston only saw 2 destroyers with his binoculars. It was a by-the-book typical PT attack. It appeared to have cost the Imperial Japanese Navy one destroyer and earned a Silver Star medal for both of the boat skippers. 72

---

[72] The Tipton Indian Daily Tribune, 2 Dec 1944

Silver Star

AWARDED FOR ACTIONS
DURING World War II

Service: Navy

Rank: Lieutenant Junior Grade

Division: Motor Torpedo Boat 497 (PT-497)

GENERAL ORDERS:

Commander 7th Fleet: Serial 01477 (April 13, 1945)

CITATION:

The President of the United States of America takes pleasure in presenting the Silver Star to Lieutenant, Junior Grade Joseph Carl Beckman, Jr. (NSN: 0-189315), United States Naval Reserve, for conspicuous gallantry and intrepidity in action as Commanding Officer of Motor Torpedo Boat FOUR HUNDRED NINETY-SEVEN (PT-497), in company with PT-492 during their attack on a Japanese Destroyer in Ormoc Bay, Philippine Islands, on 9 November 1944. Having received information that a large force of Japanese warships and transports were attempting to reinforce the Japanese positions around Ormoc Town, the boats took patrol station north of Camotes Islands, hoping to intercept and attack. At o115, Lieutenant, Junior Grade, Beckman launched his attack at the last ship in a column of three destroyers, having closed to 1,800 yards range. The two boats fired their torpedoes, and two minutes later a large explosion enveloped the Destroyer that had been attacked. Instantly the other two Destroyers placed their searchlight's beams on the two PT boats and took them under 4.7-inch fire. With greatest skill the two PT boats covered each other with smoke screens, and through blinded by the searchlights, made good their escape. Lieutenant, Junior Grade, Beckman's gallant and intrepid attack on numerically superior, high speed enemy forces, and his highly skillful evasive action were worthy of high commendation. His conduct throughout was in keeping with the highest traditions of the United States Naval Service.

PT-497 Silver Star Citation for LTJG Joseph Carl Beckman

Mike Moran's PT-494 also participated in the interdiction patrols. On December 5th He was paired with LT William H Von Bergen Jr.'s PT-531. PT-531 had not been part of the Surigao Battle. A Japanese 'Zeke' fighter bomber tried to make a kamikaze suicide attack on them. .

"At the start of this dive," Moran reported, "the plane was still under control and followed every move of PT 494. Both boats then resumed fire, very accurately. A piece was torn out of the Zeke's wing and it was seen that the Zeke was plunging straight down. PT 494 turned to the left and the Zeke crashed about 25 yards off the PT 494's starboard beam. A few parts from the plane were thrown over the bow of PT 494."[73]

PT-497 F1c (MoMM) Niel Franklin Butler obit photo ancestry.

---

[73] Bulkeley At Close Quarters p 394

PT-497 PHM1c Frank Morris Seiffert ptboatforum.com

17 Sumilon PTs PT-523, PT-524, PT-525

LCDR Francis D Tapaan, the Commander of MTBRON36, was embarked in PT-523. His trio of MTBs was assigned to cover the area off Sumilon Island. The boats of this section left their tender, USS OYSTER BAY, at around 1520 in the afternoon. They were on station at 1835 and commenced nearly 8 hours of boredom, conducting radar and visual searches of their assigned station and the approaches to it.

At 0145 PT 523 picked up a radar contact on bearing 315 at 8 miles. .At that time the boat, nicknamed 'Mustang' was traveling slowly, at 12 knots, on course 350 with mufflers closed. The target had already been reported by PT-134 of section 7. PT-523, commanded by 33 year old Robert Winfield Orrell, tracked it as moving a bit faster than previously reported. The blip resolved itself into 4 separate ships.

PT-523 22 Oct 44   NARA 80-G-372892

DIES OF WOUNDS — James David Stanley, 19, metalsmith third class, USNR, died of wounds sustained in action somewhere in the Pacific, according to a Navy Department telegram recently received by his parents, Mr. and Mrs. Fred T. Stanley of 532 West Twenty-Eighth Street. Details were not available.

A graduate of Andrew Jackson High School, where he was an outstanding football player, young Stanley entered the Navy September 1, 1943.

He had been overseas five months following indoctrination training at Norfolk, Va.

PT-523 MS3c James David Stanley   findagrave.com

Orrell, from South Carolina, was slightly older than most of the PT skippers. He had enlisted in the navy in 1929 and later had been selected for commissioning from the enlisted ranks. The common navy slang for an officer with prior enlisted service is 'Mustang'. That may be how PT-523 got her name.

When the range from PT-523 had closed to 1 1/8 miles the targets were sighted visually due to the enemy use of searchlights and star shell against section 7 and identified as 2 cruisers and 2 destroyers. PT-523 came left to course 005 in order to lead the target by about 40 degrees. At 0200 she launched her port torpedo at a range of about 2000 yards. One minute later she altered to port to course 355 and let go her second torpedo.

PT 523 LT Robert Winfield Orrell –wedding photo 1945 ancestry.com

,

Right PT-524 James Patrick Wolf   USN Midshipman School yearbook 1942

PT-524 named 'Bet Me' and commanded by James Patrick. Wolf, a former University of Texas football lineman, was located to starboard of the command boat about 75 yards away. GM3c Delman Lee Brown manned the forward gun. He was closest to the Japanese as 'Bet Me' made her approach to launch torpedoes. Gunner's Mate Walter Kundis, poised at PT 524's port torpedo rack, heard the excited Texas twang of his skipper shouting "Let's get in closer!"

Wolf was a commanding personality. He was 6' tall and everyone in the crew knew he was in charge. Walt Kundis remembered him as "One big son of a gun. There was no doubt about it – he was the boss of the boat. He was in charge. In fact when he first saw me, I was a skinny kid from Pennsylvania -- he said 'I have nothing against you. I just want to get rid of you. I want real men on my boat.' He ended up keeping me, though, and I stayed on his boat until the end, He was one good skipper. He knew how to take care of us."74

At last, Wolf gave the order to fire. No sooner .did Kundis finally pull the lanyard than the boat dipped. He lost his footing and was headed overboard when TM3c Robert Alexander Wingfield grabbed him by the belt.75 Kundis weighed in at about 124 pounds. Virginia born Bob Wingfield was only slightly larger.

PT-526 launched her port torpedo at about 0205. Skipper LTJG Donald Wheeler Hamilton Jr. used a target speed of 27 knots for the shot. After altering course as the other boats in the section had done she launched her starboard mark XIII torpedo at about 0207. PT-526 put down a brief puff of smoke as she turned to run. This smoke screen also aided to conceal the withdrawal of the other 2 boats. The three boat section retired in a column on the opposite course. The Japanese opened fire as they fled. The enemy was assumed to be using radar fire control because their shooting was quite accurate. However none of the section 6 boats returned fire and none were damaged by enemy guns.

---

74 Voices p68
75 David Sears - Wooden Boats at War History.net

While retiring another group of 5 enemy vessels following the first was detected by radar, but not visually. In any case the 3 boats had already each expended 2 fish. The section returned to its' patrol station.

The SO radar on PT-523 ceased functioning after the boat withdrew. She headed back to their assigned patrol station and soon was lying to, east of Sumilon.

At 0330 PT-524 noted 2 ships burning to the north, probably as a result of gunfire from the battleships and cruisers that were waiting for the Japanese at the north end of the straits. The same boat saw 4 columns of smoke at about 0400 located some 12 miles north of Sumilon. At 0415 the section terminated patrol and set out to return to their tender, arriving at about 1300.

PT-523 SC2c Russell Ellsworth Fish   Univ. of Washington 1930   ancestry.com

PT-523 GM3c Joshua Hannum Brooks   HS pic 1942
ancestry.com

PT-525 GM3c Chester Thomas Szot ancestry.com

PT-525 GM3c Andy Lacney findagrave.com

PT-523 BM3c Raymond Albert Romeos HS basketball 1935 – ancestry.com

Right PT-525 GM3c Walter Kundis HS photo 1942 ancestry.com

18 Lower Surigao PTs PT-490, PT-491, PT-493

Trio of PT-490, PT-491 and PT-493 were part of MTBRON 33 operating from tender OYSTER BAY. They got underway at 1530. Their station was between Kantahid Point on Dinigat Island and the eastern side of Panaon Island. The skipper of PT-490, LTJG John Mortimer ('Bus') McElfresh was the senior officer. His boat was named 'Little Butch'. The section was on station at 1900. [76]

The three boats were painted in a green and black camouflage pattern officially known as measure 21 design 20-L. All the boats of a squadron were normally painted in the same pattern, but the pattern carried by any specific squadron was not always the same as that of any other squadron. Individual boat numbers were painted in red or white on the sides of the pilot house, along with unofficial box scores of enemy craft sunk and damaged. The idea may have been copied from the aviation community where fighters had markers for air to air kills and bombers carried markers for missions completed.

---

[76] Action Report PT-490 FC8-33/A9/sq dated 30 Oct 1944 night of 24-25 Oct 1944

PT-490   ptboatforum.com

The top of the pilot house had a white star in a blue circular background for identification by friendly aircraft. Most boats also carried homemade art work depicting the name of the boat on the front of the cockpit/pilot house. PT-490 also had her number painted on the forward side of the radar mast.

PT-491   ibiblio.org

Despite the heat and humidity the crew all wore long trousers and long sleeved shirts to help protect against flash burns in combat. Every man had his own helmet. Some were marked with names or initials. On PT-490 there were special racks on the side of the dayroom for helmet storage.

PT-493 was carrying a couple of extra people. LTJG Richard Airth Hamilton, from North Dakota, had asked to ride along. He was former amateur boxer and had been exec of LTJG Joseph H. Moran's PT-494. He had been taken off that boat because; it seems, of some disagreement with his skipper. His aggressive behavior also earned him the nickname 'Dicky Dare' within MTBRON 33. The original Dicky Dare was the hero of a comic strip drawn in the 1930s by Milton Caniff. Caniff went to draw another strip after the war named 'Terry and the Pirates'. Bill Brown had a different story about Hamilton's nickname. "We always called him Dicky Dare because of his boxing background. He was a great little guy."77
One of the Squadron medics, PHM2c William Edward Gaffney Jr. had also requested a chance to go out on a 'real' combat mission.

As Bill Brown remembered it, "He was the type of kid you couldn't keep off patrol. It was hard to explain why

---

77 Voices p 104

a boat would take a corpsman out on patrol, bur Billy had to get into 78the action."79

Neither He nor Hamilton was part of the regular crew of the boat. The practice of going along for the ride was fairly common. Many individuals whose normal duties would have kept them well out of harm's way requested a chance to go, at least once, on a patrol in one of the active PT boats

PT-493 LTJG Richard Airth Hamilton A Horticulturist Goes to War.

---

[78] Voices p 104
[79] Ibid

PT-493 SC1c Anthony Paul Tatarek HS pic from 1938 ancestry.com

In PT-493, the captain, LTJG Bill Brown, left his second officer, ENS Robert E. Carter, to maintain position while he retired to the dayroom, just aft, to lie down and rest. He got up when a contact report from another section was received at about 0100. ENS Carter had been called Bob before the war. When he got to the South Pacific, he was called 'Nick', after the then popular fictional detective featured in 19th century dime novels, a 1939 movie, and a later radio series. Brown had this to say regarding his second officer "Nick was a good boat handler, so he had the wheel. I just tried to keep line of sight with the people pulling the lanyards to release the torpedoes80".

PT-491 picked up several radar contacts at 0100 off the southern tip of Panoan Island. At 0130 PT -491 made

---

[80] Voices p 109

visual contact with the group and identified the targets as 3 destroyers and a cruiser. Ten minutes later PT-490 had radar contact with the same group of approaching Japanese ships at a range of 8 miles. The enemy was heading north. A contact report was made to CTG 77.2. LTJG McElfresh formed his boats in a line of bearing with 200 yards between them. The section began a quiet approach on course 120 at 9 knots with mufflers closed. The enemy force was being tracked on radar by PT-490. Visual contact was obscured by both darkness and the intermittent rain squalls. When the enemy was about 1000 yards away the boats emerged from a rain squall and made visual sighting of the wakes of several ships. The PTs maneuvered to attack. A second enemy group of several ships was detected about 2 miles behind the first group. Later about 0430, a third group of 4 enemy ships was detected on radar heading north, and also dutifully reported to CTG 77.2.

The section continued to quietly close to a range of about 650 – 700 yards before attacking. PT-490 loosed 2 torpedoes at the lead enemy ship at 0205. Immediately after that a Japanese ship from the second group turned on a searchlight. The targeted ship also turned on a searchlight and illuminated 'Little Butch'. PT-490 opened fire on that searchlight with every gun that could be brought to bear. Meanwhile, LTJG Harley Andrew Thronson, commanding PT-491 launched 2 of his torpedoes at the second ship in the enemy column at a range of about 700 yards. The enemy ship, a destroyer, was not hit. Thronson was known in the squadron as 'Holly', probably because his first name sounded so much like it. Enemy fire was becoming intense so Holly Thronson aborted his attack. He described it like this:

"For a while we were moving in tandem with Bill Brown's 493. John McElfresh's 490 Boat was up ahead somewhere, but we really couldn't see him. I was able to get two torpedoes away. I don't know if we got a hit or not. An incoming shot blasted out the spotlight behind the cockpit, just missing Terry's head. We turned to get out of there. The Japanese ships were so close we could have bumped into one of them on the way out".81

---

[81] Voices p 109

PT-490 crew – Varallo front left, Peterson to his left
ptboatforum.com

The third PT in the section was LTJG Richard William Brown's PT-493. He was known as 'Bill', and had just celebrated his 26th birthday 2 weeks earlier. The boat was called 'Carole Baby', named for his daughter who had been born a year ago. Bill Brown had grey eyes and red hair. He also wore glasses, something unusual for a PT skipper. Brown said that Holly Thronson had been the person that made him volunteer for PT duty. The two were good friends. Thronson and Brown could have been a Mutt and Jeff comic pair. Holly was 6 feet tall while Bill, at 5'7", was one of the shorter PT skippers. But what he may have lacked in height he made up for in aggressive spirit. On this night they commanded two separate boats in the same section. 82

LTJG Richard William ('Bill') Brown   obit picture

LTJG Harley Andrew ('Holly') Thronson ancestry.com

---

82 LCDR R William Brown "They called her 'Carole Baby;'" Naval History magazine Oct 2001 p23-25

Returning to the action, John McElfresh launched his remaining two torpedoes at a range of 300-400 yards. All the torpedoes were set to run at a depth of 10 feet. His boat had been illuminated by a searchlight from one of the Japanese ships. PT-491 also launched 2 torpedoes. Both boats focused their attention, and gunfire, on the searchlight. It quickly went off, either from the gunfire or, perhaps, as the crew of PT-490 imagined, by a possible torpedo hit. A large flash was observed in the hull of the Japanese ship below the light and the searchlight was extinguished. But the flash may have come from Japanese guns.

PT-490 was subjected to a stream of heavy, and accurate, enemy fire. The enemy fire was being returned by the PT gunners. TM3c Arthur George Peterson from Chicago manned the starboard twin fifty machine guns. TM3c Anthony John Baptist Varallo from Kankakee, Illinois was on the port side pair.

One Japanese shell punched a hole in the wooden hull above the waterline on the starboard side, forward. Another tore off her own small searchlight. PT-490's VHF radio was put out of commission. The only man injured was 18 year old TM3c Arthur Peterson. He was knocked down when shell fragments from the first Japanese rounds hit him in the head. Despite his wounds Bud Peterson made his way aft to open the TiCl4 smoke canister.83 Bus McElfresh turned his boat sharply to port and began laying smoke as he attempted to withdraw.

Terry Chambers, at the wheel of PT-490 remembered "Somehow we'd gotten inside their destroyer screen. We were facing big ships and all we could do was aim our guns at the lights and the ships' bridges, like sticking our fingers in their eyes. We'd knock one light out and another went on."84

Thronson's boat, named 'Devil's Daughter', also turned away and began laying smoke. And lost contact with the other boats while doing so. Before contact was lost lookouts in Devils Daughter reported an enemy ship was apparently on fire. Inside PT-490's pilot house QM3c Albert Lee ('Al') McCready from Portland OR struggled to keep a record of everything that was happening around them.

PT-493 had made her attack approach on a course slightly to left of that of her sisters. It appears she was not detected at the same time as PT-490. ENS Robert E. Carter, the 22 year old second officer, conned the boat

---

83 Breuer – Devil Boats p 188
84 Voices p 109

to within about 500 yards of the Japanese ships. Bill Brown ordered his crew to prepare to launch two torpedoes. At the same time, the Japanese picked up on her and began intense, and accurate, gunfire at 'Carole Baby'.

"We ended up firing three torpedoes" Brown said, "A piece of shrapnel got imbedded in the hull and jammed the fourth fish in the rack. I ordered Nick to turn hard left, open throttles, and get out. I ran aft to turn on the smoke generator."85

Carter turned the boat hard to port, opened the mufflers, and increased power to full throttle on all three engines. The last torpedo, on the starboard side, aft, was the one that had failed to release properly. The skipper aborted the torpedo attack and 'Carole Baby' turned sharply to port. Japanese searchlights and star shells lit up the attacking PTs almost as if it were daylight.

"I could even read the dials on my watch." Bill Brown recalled.86

Ted Gurzynski in the port side twin fifties mount put it like this. "The Japanese broke out searchlights and star

---

85 ibid
86 Voices p 109

shells. They found us, lights so bright you thought you were on stage." All the guns on 'Carole Baby' that could be brought to bear began firing at the searchlights. Ted continued "(They) started to fire at us. By then we were firing too." 87

At about 0220, when PT-493 was first hit by enemy gunfire. PT-490 plunged through the screen laid by PT-493 and headed away at high speed.

Bill Brown in PT 493 received a report from MoMM2c Alfred W. ('Al') Brunelle, his engine room watch stander, that one Japanese shell had come through the wooden side of the boat above the waterline on the port side, traveled through the engine room, smashed some machinery, including a generator, and exited below the waterline on the starboard side without exploding. A second shell followed a similar path through the lazarette compartment aft of the engine room. Brunelle cut all the circuit breakers and climbed over to where the enemy shell had exited the engine room. He stuffed his kapok life jacket in the hole to slow the flooding. As he put it "I used my head instead of my body".88

---

[87] Ibid
[88] Voices p 110

Brunelle then climbed back and nursed the engines to keep them running while 'Carolle Baby' tried to escape. This activity would later be recognized by the award of a Navy Cross, the service's second highest medal for heroism.

MoMM2c Ted Gurzynski with a generic PT service patch

Albert Brunelle, PT 493

MoMM2c Albert W. J. ('Al') Brunelle

19 year old RM2c William Sekerak, a native of Cleveland, Illinois, called to his captain from inside the charthouse to report that the radio had lost power and was not functioning. That isn't surprising since the hit in the engine room had disabled the generator. Bill Sekerak headed aft to see about restoring power to his radio. Five minutes later, at 0225, the third enemy shell struck the radar mast just aft of the chart house. This one exploded and sprayed shrapnel over the entire area. One of the passengers, 23 year old PHM2c Billy Gaffney, had been on deck forward of the pilot house on the starboard side. He was mortally wounded. The two regular officers, LTJG Brown and ENS Carter, were knocked down by the blast and suffered wounds. The volunteer third officer, LTJG Hamilton, was

wounded in the face. His nose and lip were both cut and bleeding, but he wasn't out of action. The gunner on the port side 20mm, 22 year old SC1c Anthony Paul Tatarek, received a large number of pieces of shrapnel. Tony Tatarek was the ships cook. His being on the 20mm gun was another example of how PT sailors often did double duty in roles other than the one they were originally trained to fill. Another example was MoMM2c Theodore Stanley Gurzynski from Milwaukee, WI, the leading engineer. Ted Gurzynski said ""I never wanted to be in there when we were in any action. I thought I had a better chance of coming out alive if I was topside, I was the senior motor mac, so I told the other two if they stood engine watch when we went out, I'd stand watch there all the way back to the base", So he was placed, at his own request, as the gunner on the port side twin 0.50 89machine gun mount. 90
Ted Gurzynski only took some shrapnel in his hands, but he saw, or rather no longer saw, Billy Gaffney. Gaffney's body was thrown into the inside lower compartment.

"Billy was standing right there at the rack when the shell hit." Ted said, "He was killed instantly, blown right out of his shoes. Just the way he stood there, that's the way those shoes were. They didn't even turn over."91

____

[90] Voices p67
[91] Voices p109-110

The skipper only had flash burns, [92]but Tony Tatarek was very badly injured in the stomach. Other crewmembers carried him below, but he expired within a very short time.

 When Bill Brown recovered he headed aft to ensure the valves on the Titanium Tetrachloride smoke screen bottles were open.

'Carole Baby' was seriously hurt. Al Brunelle had tried to plug the hole in her hull, but water was still coming in. He managed to keep the engines running and the boat maintained a 25 knot speed while escaping. Nick Carter pointed the boat towards Panoan Island. He found a spot where he could get closer to the shore as the sea water level in the engine room continued to rise. At about 0245 the bow of the boat hit the shore, just about when the engines finally ceased responding. Skipper Brown organized his crew for an orderly abandonment of their boat. The first crew members took weapons from the armory and they waded ashore. The last men off carried the bodies of their dead comrades, Gaffney and Tatarek.

Crew members with weapons were positioned to form a defensive perimeter for the improvised beachhead

---

[92] Voices p 110

while LTJG R. A. Hamilton and Chief Quartermaster J. J. Gagliardi returned to the boat to destroy all classified publications and equipment. When PT-491 arrived, the survivors moved off the beach to be rescued. Again, they brought the bodies of their fallen shipmates with them.

At 0530, PT-491 was alone. She had lost contact with the other boats at around 0245 while desperately maneuvering to escape from Japanese gunfire. She now sighted a burning Japanese cruiser. Holly Thronson tried to report the contact. The attempt was not successful. The blue eyed skipper from Wisconsin started to make an approach. But the Japanese detected his boat and began to fire on it. With enemy 8" shells exploding around him 6 foot tall Holly launched his remaining 2 torpedoes. The range was 3000 yards. The target was seen to turn and the torpedoes missed. The boat's second officer, Californian ENS Terry Chambers, once again swiftly conned PT-491 away from enemy gunfire.

While returning to their home tender a formation of 4 Japanese Aichi type 99 (Val) dive bombers encountered PT-490. The first pair of dive bombers each dropped a bomb. Both missed PT-490 by about 200 yards. The second pair veered away, deterred by defensive fire. PT-490 fired a total of 125 rounds of 40mm, 45 rounds of

37mm, 120 rounds of 20mm, and 2200 rounds of 0.50 caliber at the aircraft and the searchlights.

PT-491 Holly Thronson and Terry Chambers
ptboatforum.com

PT-491 was headed north at about 0645 when her crew sighted PT-493 beached off Maoyo Point. The camouflage coloring of a dark green stripe on a lighter green background made it difficult to identify their damaged squadron mate. PT-493 could only be seen using binoculars from about 2 miles away. While picking up the crew of PT-493 another section of MTBRON 33 boats arrived on the scene. This trio, PTs 489, 495 and

497, escorted Holly Thronson's PT-491 and her load of survivors back to San Pedro Bay, arriving at around 1030.

PT-493 slipped off the reef with the rising tide and sank beneath the surface. The crew members that were brought back to the tender were given Survivor's leave of 30 days in the US. This was a standard award to crew members of any ship that was sunk by enemy action during most of the war.

PT-493, wreck   from They called
Her Carole Baby USNIP

19 Upper Surigao PTs PT-327, PT-326, PT-321

LT Carl Thomas Gleason from Lowell, Massachusetts, commanded the group assigned to cover the NE corner of the strait. Carl was 34 years old. He was a former enlisted sailor appointed LTJG on May1, 1943. LT Gleason was now in command of MTBRON 21 His boats were painted green overall. He was assigned to lead the 3 boats on patrol on the NE side of Surigao Straight. Their station was defined as being 4 miles West of Kanihaan Island. That station was one of the furthest from where the tenders had set up shop. His boats departed from their tender, USS OYSTER BAY, at 1535 on Oct 24th.

Gleason rode in ENS Kenneth B Sharpe's PT-327 known as 'Hell's Half Acre'. Just before he completed MTB school and knew he was headed into the war zone Sharpe wrote a letter to his Aunt Marion Sharpe Daughaday in which he said "Of all my friends I have who have been in uniform long before I have, I will be the first to get into the fight out in the battle area just my luck.".

PT-321 rescuing Japanese survivors   Navsource
120532101

Sharpe, who had been captain of his high school
football team, got a subscription to Readers Digest from
his aunt the Christmas before he headed to the South
Pacific. He was a great fan of that magazine.

PT-327 Kenneth Bell Sharpe   from Dave Whelan

PT-326 Howard L. Terry   terryfoundation.org

The second boat in the section was PT-326 under ENS Howard Lindsey Terry from Alabama.

"We didn't know exactly what was coming at us but we knew that there were a lot of big Japanese ships coming our way." Terry related.

"There were about 33 of us deployed in groups of three all along the Strait. Our orders were to report the movements of the ships and to try and make torpedo runs to harass them or disable them", he continued, "My friend Jackson Hinds, a supply officer on one of the PT boat tenders, requested permission to come along on our mission and was granted permission to accompany us.".93

JACKSON C. HINDS, JR.
Ensign
Single   Age: 22
HOUSTON, TEXAS
University of Texas, B.B.A., 1942,
Harvard Business School, I.A.,
1943.
Beta Gamma Sigma, Phi Delta
Phi.
Student.

ENS Jackson Ceivers Hinds Jr.   Navy Supply School Officers Course

---

93 Cotham, A PT Skipper in the Pacific p 11

PT-326's second officer was Robert Brandt Rardin, nicknamed Pete, a former Rochester U medical student from Portsmouth, Ohio. After the war ended he would complete his medical studies, for now, there was a war to fight.

PT-326 Robert Brant Rardin – Young American Patriots

PT-327 Gordon Steadman Samble from Susan Lavigne
ancestry.com

One of the newest additions to the crew was F1c Bazil
Offner Layman from West Virginia. Bud Layman was just
19 years old and fresh from navy schools on the Packard
engines that drove the boats. After his initial training he
had been sent to the South Pacific as an individual crew
replacement on board the transport USS GENERAL
JOHN POPE (AP-110). He joined PT-326 on September
24th, 1944.After the war he would return home, attend
a local college, marry, and raise a family. Now he was
just a green kid about to get his first taste of a real war.
Brown eyed RM3c Joseph Louis Stefanofski from NY was
trained to handle radio communications for PT-326; He
frequently was stationed as a machine gunner.

PT 321, 'Death's Hand', commanded by five foot ten inch ENS Louis E. Thomas was the third boat of the trio. ENS Robert William Milliron from Pennsylvania was his second officer. All three of the above PTs were on station by 1830. They then lay to and waited. At about 0300 PT-321 made radar contact with approaching enemy ships. The targets were about 10 miles to the South and were tracked as heading North at 20 knots. This was reported to LT Gleason at 0305. PT-326 also made contact on the same group of targets. The contacts were reported via PT-327 to COMDESRON54 who was located a bit further to the North. He, in turn, told the PTs to remain clear because he was preparing to attack with his destroyers and did not want potential interference.94

LTJG Terry, the skipper of PT-326, said "One of my crew pointed with amazement at the edge of the radar screen and said 'Captain, that isn't an island. It's moving. That's a ship.'".95

The troubles for this trio started soon after. First the generator on PT-327 failed at about 0330. This left her without radar. PT-326 lost her radar about a half an hour later. The main American battle line was already

____

[94] Action Report PT-327 30 Oct, 1944 FC8-21/A16-3/jak
[95] Cotham p 11

delivering massive amounts of gunfire aimed at the oncoming Japanese and around 0415 boats from the group finally began to creep forward in order to make torpedo attacks. The target was a Japanese Destroyer that was burning and had a second ship close by.

MoMM1c Gordon Steadman Samble, a 21 year old from Jacksonville, FL, was in charge of the engine room. Samble had enlisted in the regular navy in July 1941 in Macon, Georgia. He had then been sent to school on PT engines, and after that to MTB School at Melville, RI. Samble was sent to the South Pacific as a replacement on board USS SIRIUS (AK-15) and reported to MTBRON 21 on April 8th, 1944.He, personally, managed to get the generator running again. 96 The skipper, ENS Sharpe, commended him for doing an excellent job. After the action, on November First, Gordon Samble extended his enlistment for another two years. 97 Samble had played in the school orchestra in high school. Keeping the Packard gasoline engines humming was just making a different kind of music.

At 0450 LT Gleason's three PTs made attack runs. The Japanese detected them and began firing at them. The first shots were not accurate, but those that followed

---

[96] Action Report PT-327 30 Oct, 1944 FC8-21/A16-3/ jak
[97] Muster roll MTBRON 21, November 1944

came closer and closer. PT-327 launched 2 torpedoes at a range of about 4000 yards. She then turned tail and opened her throttles to get away as fast as she could. The 80 foot long wooden boats were not designed to withstand gunfire.

Howard Terry, commanding PT-326, described it like this: "As we got within a few thousand yards the secondary batteries on the big Japanese ships opened up and it looked like a solid wall of fire ahead of you. You just knew that nothing could survive in there. And here we were going at them in a plywood boat. I'll never forget that moment. I turned to my friend Jackson Hinds and said 'I'm sorry' and he said 'Why's that?' 'Because I think I've gotten you killed,' I replied."[98]

PT-326 released one torpedo when she was about 3500 yards from her target and then followed the command boat while laying a smoke screen of TiCl4 gas.

PT-321 was making her approach at 6 knots when the Japanese opened fire on the section. She was preparing to release her torpedo but the cable holding it to deck became stuck. Brown eyed S1c Kenneth Eugene Parker from Bloomington moved to free the cable and was injured by shrapnel just at that moment. The enemy

---

[98] Cotham p 11

shell struck the radar mast and made a hole. Parker was knocked down, but still trying to reach the torpedo, which remained on deck and whose motor was running full speed. He almost slid overboard but GM3c George Rizen who was 6' 1" tall was able to grab him by the belt and pull him away from the side. Rizen was just 18 years old. The executive officer, ENS R W Milliron, and 5' 7" GM2c John Kuhar managed to throw the torpedo over the side. Meanwhile, the skipper swung the boat around and retired while zig-zagging to avoid enemy fire. [99]

Once clear, PT-326 came alongside PT-321 and the exec of 326 jumped across to 321. That officer was 26 year old ENS Pete Rardin, who had left medical school to go to fight. His earlier training allowed him to administer plasma that probably saved Seaman Parker's life.

The main battle line of battleships and cruisers engaged the approaching Japanese by hurling a massive amount of shells at them. The PTs cleared away from the gun battle. By 0539 it was all over and Rear Admiral Oldendorf, the overall commander, was able to cease fire and order his ships to go after survivors. "Do not overload your ships with survivors. Search each man

---

[99] Action Report PT-327 30 Oct, 1944 FC8-21/A16-3/jak

well to see that he does not have any weapons. Anyone offering resistance—shoot him. Proceed independently to pick up survivors."100

Gleason's PTs joined in this effort as seen in the photo on page 129. The Japanese destroyer ASAGUMO had rescued men from the battleship FUSO when FUSO sank earlier. Now ASAGUMO was sunk. Among the survivors were the Captain, CDR Kazuo Shibayama IJN, and his chief engineer, LT Tokichi Ishii. In a later interview CDR Shibayama gave the mosquito boats a compliment, "It sank so fast. Most miserable. American PTs too fast."

Left PT-326 F1c Bazil Offner ('Bud') Layman -Obit photo timeswv.com

---

100 Warfarehistorynetwork.com

PT-321 GM2c Paul Joseph Vinci with tattoo. This picture was included to show another example of tattooing that was so common among PT sailors. Vinci was transferred away from MTBRON 21 prior to the Surigao Strait battle

PT-321 ENS Louis Emile Thomas in 1938 as fullback at Tulane ancestry.com

20 Kanihaan PTs PT-495, PT-492, PT-489.

The section on the northeast corner of the PT patrol areas was assigned to MTBRON33. The Squadron commander himself, 31 year old LT Arthur Murray Preston, led this section in PT-495. The squadron voice radio call sign was 'Clown', and LT Preston was called 'Clown Leader'. But there was nothing funny about their mission tonight. The boats were to operate around ¼ mile south of Kanihaan Island. The lead boat was commanded by Philadelphian LTJG Frank Hastings Olton, who was actually a couple of years older than the squadron commander. The other 2 vessels were PT-492, under LT Melvin Wolf Haines from Chicago, and PT-489, skippered by ENS Herbert A. Gregg, whose wife, Virginia, was a corporal in the Marine Corps. The second officer of PT-492 was Paul M Stoneback. During the war he grew a moustache like movie star Erroll Flynn.

LTJG Paul Milton Stoneback   ancestry.com

ENS Stoneback as XO of PT-492 ptboatforum.com

LCDR Arthur M Preston   NH106427

LT Preston had previously been awarded a Navy Cross for moving his boat close to shore off the New Guinea coast on a volunteer mission to rescue ENS Harold

Thompson, an F6F Hellcat pilot whose fighter plane had been brought down by Japanese fire. This action took place prior to the PT boat redeployment to the Philippines; Preston had volunteered to attempt the rescue along with the intelligence officer, LT Don Seaman. They rode in two boats; Preston's PT-498, skippered by LTJG Wilfred Benjamin Tatro Jr., and PT-363 under the command of LTJG Hershel F. Boyd. All the crews were volunteers because this was an extremely hazardous rescue mission. The two PTs were under fire from shore batteries PT-489 made the run in to pick up the wounded aviator wile PT-363 provided cover. ENS Thompson needed help. LT Seaman and MoMM1c Charles D. Day (predictably nicknamed 'Happy') jumped into the bay to hoist Hal Thompson up. With everyone safely back aboard, the two PTs left the scene as fast as possible. They had been under fire for about 2 and a half hours. CDR Bowling, in charge of all Seventh Fleet MTBs, recommended Preston for the Medal of Honor. Staff officers up the chain of command reduced the award to a Navy Cross. Biff Bowling was never pleased with that decision, and when he returned to the USA he used his Naval Academy contacts to lobby for reevaluating the award. He was successful. Preston's award was upgraded to the Medal of Honor. The presentation of the nation's highest award for bravery was made by President Truman after Preston had returned to the US. Other participants also were also decorated for this rescue. LT Seaman got a Navy Cross, as did Tatro, Boyd, and Day. Tatro also got a purple heart and a ticket home because the wounds he had received were severe.

LCDR Preston receiving MOH from President Truman
Navsource 1212054801

PT-489 being restored and marked as PT-109
Navsource 120548902

PT-495   ibiblio.org/hyperwar/USN/ships/PT/PT-495

The 3 boats were all from MTBRON 33. The squadron had a lot of individual variations in armament on the boats. For example: All the boats carried 2 depth charges aft of their smoke generator bottle except for PT-495. She had 2 TiCL4 bottles and carried no Depth Charges.PT-493 carried her 2 depth charges on the side, between the torpedoes. Squadron 33 boats had improvised a special mount for one of their 20mm forward guns. It combined the 20mm with a 0.50 caliber M2 machine gun. They called it an 'Acey-Deucy', after a popular variation of backgammon. The term is also used in horse racing where a jockey may intentionally ride with one stirrup shorter than the other to gain better balance on turns. The squadron boats carried 3 20mm mounts forward. On PT-495 the combined mount was on the starboard side. On PT-489 and PT-493 it occupied the center position. PT-495 also had an extra pair of 0.30 cal. Machine guns on the wings of the cockpit. Most boats had only one such gun. All the boats carried their 40mm army style gun aft on the deck, without a platform and without pipe rails to prevent the gun from being able to aim into the boat's own structure.

The trio of PTs departed from their tender, OYSTER BAY, at 1530 and arrived on station at 1815. At that time they-lay to and conducted a radar search. Their station was quite a distance from the entrance to Surigao Strait, so they just waited, watched, and listened. At 0010 they heard PT-127 report contacts south of Bohol. And about 50 minutes later they saw gun flashes and searchlight glare bearing 215, over southern part of Panaon.

Finally, at 0315, they acquired a radar contact on 1 Japanese battleship, bearing 260 at 6 miles distance and moving slowly north. The section began closing this target. At 0323 visual contact was made at a range of 3 miles. Just a few minutes later COMDESRON54 reported he was closing from the north so LT Preston abandoned the chase and maneuvered to remain clear. The PTs were back on station at 0340. Within 5 minutes they could see the target was on fire. When their patrol took them past the location, at 0645, they only found only a burning patch of oil.

At 0400 they saw a destroyer, bearing 300, range 4 miles, also aflame, and a few minutes later they detected 2 more destroyers bearing 240 range 4 miles that were also burning. These were Japanese ships being dealt with by the main body of the American force. The PTs remained out of the action. The first fire disappeared after about 30 minutes.

At 0600 the radio picked up a call for help from PT-491, She had located the badly damaged PT-493.

They made another visual sighting south of Panoan at around 0650 at a range of about 7 miles. It was identified as a Mogami class heavy cruiser proceeding south at high speed and burning aft. Again, no attempt was made to attack because heavier American forces were known to be in pursuit.

An explosion was felt at 0735, probably from one of the other destroyers sinking. When the group headed for home at 0830 there was nothing afloat where the targets had been.

The summary for this trio of boats was that they had been observers on the sidelines and had not fired a single shot in anger. And this was not because they lacked fighting spirit. Most of the crew of PT-495 had been together since December, 1943, when the squadron was commissioned. But two of them; S2c Raymond Lemos Wilbur Jr. and MoMM2c Ralph Aldrich Sunderhauf, had just joined the boat less than a month ago. Wilbur was just 18 years old. He and 4 others were still teen-agers. The others in the PT-495 crew were in their early twenties.

On the night of November 19th/20th three MTBRON33 boats were out together on a mission to attack Japanese barges in Ormoc Bay. LT Olton was in command. The boats were: PT-495, PT-491 and PT-489. A Japanese plane attacked them as they withdrew and placed a fragmentation bomb alongside PT-495. RM2c Alonzo Louis Clayton from Illinois was killed. He was initially buried in plot #1, grave #5 in the military cemetery on Panoan Island. There were 7 others who were wounded. That included both of the newcomers,

Ray Wilbur and Dick Sunderhauf, QM2 Park Joseph Smith, Cox Anthony Torres, MoMM3c Claude Greenwell, MoMM3c Denver Lowell ('Chicken Little') , and TM2c Elmer Earl ('Marty') Martin. The wounded were initially sent to LST-1025, a standard 325 foot tank landing ship that had been converted to act as a hospital ship during landing operations. They were transferred again, this time to a real hospital ship, USS HOPE (AH-7), for further treatment and a voyage back to the US.

The cook for PT-495 was Lawrence Buell Crenshaw. At battle stations the blue eyed Kentuckian was a gunner. He divorced his first wife before joining the Navy and had married Alline Agnes Presley on January 29th, 1943, before going overseas to war with MTBRON 33.

PT-495 MoMM2c Denver Lowell Thurman   Owensboro KY Messenger Inquirer 29 Sep 2012 p C2

Ailine Agnes Presley & Lawrence Buel Crenshaw wedding picture
January 29, 1943

PT-495 SC2c Lawrence Buell Crenshaw wedding picture
findagrave.com

Among the 17 wounded in this same action were:

QM2 Park Joseph Smith, who was born in Ohio in 1922. He would find himself back with MTBRON 33 in about 6 months.

MoMM2 Ralph Aldrich Sunderhauf, a 6 foot tall 26 year old from San Diego, California.

MoMM2 Denver Lowell Thurman, another 6 foot tall Kentuckian. He was nicknamed 'Chicken Little'.101

---

[101] Louisville KY Courier and Press 1 Oct 2009

Coxswain Anthony Torres from Michigan. The rating of Coxswain was a holdover from an earlier era. It would soon be renamed BM3c (Boatswains mate 3rd class)

S1c(TM) Raymond Lemos Wilbur, who was only 19 years old, had just reported aboard on September 28th, 1944. Ray Wilbur's participation in the fighting war had lasted less than 2 months.

TM2c Edward Joseph Stevens, a 22 year old torpedoman with an eagle tattoo on his left arm. The popular image of sailors with tattoos came from the fact that about 65% of enlisted sailors in World War II had them. Stevens was the only one listed here to be transferred to an overseas base hospital.

All of the other men mentioned above were injured badly enough to warrant transfer to the nearby hospital ship USS HOPE for further treatment and subsequent transfer to the US. They had survived the big battle in Surigao Strait unscathed, but there was still a war on and, for most, their part in it had just ended. All of them were awarded the Purple Heart.

Into the Jaws of Death

PT-495 S2c Ray Wilbur

PT-495 MoMM2c Ralph Aldrich Sunderhauf HS photo
1937

PT-495 MoMM2c Claude Greenwell on engine room hatch ptboatforum.com

PT-495 TM2c Elmer Earl Martin obit ancestry.com

21 S Amagusan Point PTs PT-320, PT-330, PT-331

LT George Walter Martin Hogan Jr. commanded PT-320 of MTBRON 21. He led a three boat section that had what was possibly the least exciting patrol of the battle. His section launched no torpedoes and made no sighting reports. Their assigned patrol area was off South Amugasan Point, near the northern limit of the PT patrol areas. The other 2 boats were PT-330 under LTJG Emmette Reeks from New Orleans, and PT-331 commanded by ENS William P West. Both West and Reeks, along with the future skipper of PT-323, Herb Stadler, had arrived in the South Pacific together on board the navy cargo ship USS GANYMEDE in July.

Neither the radar on PT-330, named 'Balzonal', nor the radar on PT-320, named 'Sea Bitch', were performing well. But PT-331 ('Ramblin' Wrecker') made several radar contacts. The group was located in close proximity to the main battle force and could hear how much radio traffic was being sent on the voice circuits. They were also aware that any data they had from their own observations had already been reported. The moon had set at 1818 and visibility in the dark was limited to, at best, a mere 2 miles. Frequent rain squalls did nothing to improve visual detection ranges. When the section started to maneuver into a possible attack position the radio traffic let them know that the 'big boys' were already engaging those targets. The section was reduced to the role of sideline observer, and contributed nothing.102

PT-331   Navsource 120533101

PT-330   Navsource 120533001

---

102 PT-320 Action Report FC8-21/AI6-3/jak 30 Oct 1944

PT-330 skipper Emmette Reeks as a junior at LSU in 1939

The second officer in PT-320 was LTJG Samuel Eveleth Badger Jr. At 32, Sam Badger was one of the oldest men in the squadron. Service in the mosquito boats was definitely for young men. Nearly half of the crew of the Sea Bitch was still in their teens. The longest serving member was QM3c William Harold Youngs. He had been aboard since May, less than 6 months earlier. Several of the crew received advancements in rate in order to fill a vacant position on the boat. Navy Bureau of Personnel Circular letter 144-44 authorized this step and reduced the required time the sailors had to have served in their previous grade by as much as fifty per cent. Beneficiaries included GM3c Vernon Manley, S1c (RM) James McDonald, and TM1c Thomas Bennett. MoMM1c Norman Sparrow was transferred in on

October 8th to provide an experienced head of the engine room crew. The other engineers were F1c Joseph Farnese, F1c Russell McKinney, and F1c Warren Watson. Similarly, Tom Bennet was transferred in to be senior torpedoman on September 3rd. S1c George Petrulavage was another newcomer. He reported aboard on September 19th.The crews of all the PTs had similar stories. 103 The Navy Bureau of Personnel tried to honor their commitment to have men assigned to PT boats to spend no more than a year in combat overseas before rotating them back to the states for other duty, often as instructors for new men.

The boats were designed for the crews to eat, sleep, and fight, especially the latter. An assignment like the one they were now on did not leave much room for eating and sleeping, either. Weather in the Philippines is usually hot and humid. There is also little difference in temperature between day and night in October.

These 3 PTs remained near their patrol station until about 0645. At that time they set course for their home base. PT-328 and PT-429 joined them. At about 0915 the group was attacked by Japanese aircraft and all responded with fire from their gun batteries. PT-330

---

[103] Muster rolls MTBRON21 Sep-Dec 1944

even thought they had scored a hit on one plane with a 40mm round, and several more with their .30 and .50 caliber machine guns. But the Japanese planes were not destroyed.

Japanese aircraft got their revenge about 10 days later, on November 5th. A bomb from one of them scored a direct hit on PT-320 while she was nested alongside her mother tender, USS WACHAPREAGUE (AGP 8). The boat was a total wreck. All her officers and crew were killed except for TM1c Tom Bennett.

Bill Youngs was 2 weeks shy of his 22nd birthday. Farnese was also almost 22. Sparrow and Petrulavage were 21. The others, except for Mcdonald, were under 20, with Manley being the youngest. He had not yet celebrated his 18th birthday.

The full casualty list from PT-320:

26 year old LT George Walter Martin Hogan Jr. from Chicago IL   KIA

23 year old LTJG Samuel Eveleth ('Sam') Badger Jr. from Groton MA   KIA

18 year old S1c (GM) Donald ('Don') Adler from Everett WA MIA

21 year old F1c Joseph Michael ('Joe') Farnese from Coraopolis PA   MIA

19 year old S1c Albin James Kremzar from Cleveland OH KIA

17 year old GM3c Vernon Arthur Manley from Flint MI KIA

24 year old S2c (RM) James Joseph McDonald from Springfield MA   MIA

18 year old F1c Russell Harry McKinney Jr. from Detroit MI MIA

21 year old S1c George Petrulavage from Boston MA KIA

21 year old MoMM1c Norman Raymond Sparrow from Indianapolis IN KIA

18 year old S1c Donald Lincoln Stockwell from Buffalo NY KIA

18 year old S1c Keith Leroy Walkington from De Smet SD KIA

21 year old QM3 William Harold ('Bill') Youngs from Wake Forest IL   KIA

21 year old TM1c Thomas Leslie ('Tom') Bennett from Timber OR   WIA

Not all the bodies were recovered. Four of the men were initially listed as Missing in Action. The initial telegram to next of kin is a cold and impersonal notification. The Jewish Welfare Board regularly arranged for a visit to the families by a group that included an officer and a clergyman to explain whatever rights and benefits were due as well as to put a more human face on the report. In the case of Donald Adler, Jewish Welfare Board records indicate there may have been two visits; one when he was declared missing, and another when he was declared Killed in Action. It caught my attention specifically because Donald Adler was not Jewish.104

The sole survivor of the PT-320 crew, Tom Bennett, was originally taken to the hospital ship USS HOPE (AH-7). Once the doctors had given him clearance to travel he was embarked in an attack transport, USS LAPORTE (APA-151) for the voyage back to the states.

Ancestry.com WWII Jewish Welfare Board cards

Wreckage of PT-320 alongside WACHAPREAGUE (AGP 8)
NH44321

PT-320, the Sea Bitch, had survived her part in the
greatest naval battle ever fought only to be reduced to
a floating pile of splintered scrap wood just days later.
The young men that sailed in her came through that
battle unscathed. But they would be cut down in one of
the myriad of small, nameless, violent, encounters that
encompass the reality of war.

PT-320 officers Sam Badger and George Hogan
ptboatforum.com

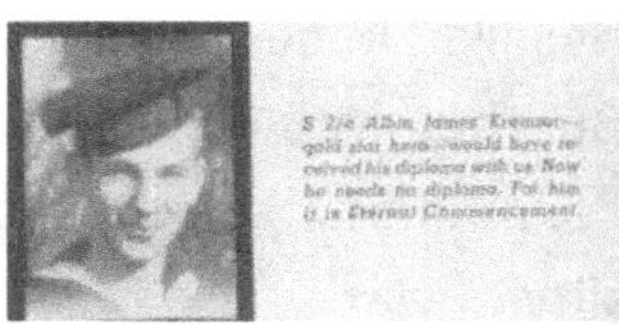

PT-320 S2c Albin James Kremzar   HS yearbook

PT-320 LTJG Sam E. Badger East Orange NJ HS Yearbook 1929

PT-320 QM3c William Harold ('Bill') Youngs kaconnoly on ancestry.com

PT-320 S1c Donald Adler   HS Yearbook photo 1944 His nickname in High School was 'Happy' and his ambition on graduation was to join the Navy.

PT-320 F1c Joseph Michael ('Joe') Farnese   Coraopolis PA HS Yearbook

22 E Amagusan Point PTs PT-323, PT-328, PT-329

The 3 boats assigned to patrol the sector East of Amugasan Point also had a very quiet night. That is to say that for most of the time they were not very active. The commander of the sector was LTJG Howard Grier Young. He rode in PT-328. His boat, named 'Bayonne Bitch', was accompanied by PT-329 ('Hell's Belle') under the command of LTJG John Lester Mee, and PT-323 ('Calamity Jane') skippered by LTJG Herbert Stadler.

The three boats left together at a little after 1500. They reached their patrol station some 4 hours later and settled down to a routine of combined visual and radar watch. The routine was completely boring; nothing to report, nothing to do, and no relief from the hot and humid weather. The heat and humidity were particularly oppressive because the crews wore long trousers and long sleeved shirts while out on a combat mission. During a normal day alongside their tender the men wore shorts and often no shirt at all.

October in the Philippines meant an average temperature of around 80 degrees Fahrenheit and relative humidity to match. There was plenty of rain. October in the Philippines usually means rain on 2 out of every 3 days. The temperature and humidity did not vary much even at night.

PT 328 in measure 31 - 20L   Navsource 120532801

The boats moved a bit to the north to counter the effect of the current flowing through the strait. The radar on PT-328 was not working. Then the 3 boats lay to. PT-323 recorded a pair of destroyers passing heading south. Several minutes later the destroyers passed again, this time going north. These destroyers were USS MONSSEN and USS McDERMUT of DESDIV 108. PT-328 saw them, too, and identified them as being US Fletcher class destroyers. Commander Destroyer Division 108 had previously warned the PTs that he was proceeding down the strait to make his attack. A few minutes later, the flagship, PT-328, noted there was gunfire to the south, somewhere inside the strait. About 15 minutes later all three boats noted star shells and the beam of a searchlight could be seen to the south east. The searchlight beam swept across the three PTs, came to rest for a few seconds on PT-328, and then was turned off. The three boats maneuvered to avoid the beam, and in so doing, lost visual contact with one another. From this point on each boat had a story of its' own.

On 'Hell's Belle', the lookouts spotted a destroyer trailing heavy black smoke passing from the south east. The crew went to battle alert and prepared for a torpedo attack on the strange vessel. No attack was actually made because there was a chance that the potential target was friendly. When the target moved away, Jack Mee realized he had lost contact with his group. From then on, PT-329 was unable to make radio contact with anyone.105

---

[105] PT-329 Action Report FC8-21/AI6-3/jak 30 Oct 1944

PT-329 S1c (QM) William Herald Ferguson
ptboatforum.com

PT-329 ENS John Lester Mee – wedding picture
ancestry.com

PT-328 Howard G Young as commander of company 61
at Columbia University Midshipman School in 1943
from school yearbook 'Side Boy'

PT-323 TM2c Richard Francis Lowe findagrave.com

The 'Bayonne Bitch' went through the same drill. Her
radar had ceased to function so she had to rely on visual
sightings. After aborting her potential attack she retired
around Amugasan Point. Soon after that, she fell in with
another group of four PTs; PT-320, PT-330, PT-331, and
PT-489. These 5 remained together for their return to

base. En route they were attacked by Japanese aircraft at around 0915. PT-328 fired 27 rounds of 40mm, 35 rounds of 37mm, 50 rounds of 20mm, and 1000 rounds of .50 cal. at the attacking planes. There was no evidence that the gunfire did any damage. The Japanese dropped 2 bombs. These also had no effect.

'Calamity Jane' briefly came under attack. Two large caliber shells were aimed at her when she was about a mile northeast of Amugasan Point. . One burst on a hill off the port quarter, over a mile away. But the second was much closer. The explosion, about 50 yards off the port quarter, lifted the stern of the boat out of the water. Everyone felt it. There was nothing more, and the boat was not damaged.

PT-329 logged a visual sighting of 3 oil fires; bearing 150, range about 9 miles at 0400. It was probably originally written down by S1c Bill Ferguson from Illinois. About a half hour later her radar picked up a contact in Cabilian Bay that turned out to be a friendly patrol boat. LTJG Jack Mee took his boat around Amugasan Point and lay to near the shore until about 0600. Then he headed his boat home. At about 0830 5 Japanese aircraft flew by and PT-329 fired at them with her 40mm, 20mm, and .50 caliber guns, but failed to hit.

At 0920 she joined PT-492 and PT-495 for the remainder of the trip back to tender OYSTER BAY.

The only PT with 2 Jewish officers was PT-323. LTJG Herbert Stadler was skipper. ENS William Ira Adelman was XO. Adelman graduated from Harvard in 1936 and joined his father's family business, a lumber yard in Pittsburgh. He married Meryl June Ruben in 1940.They had two children under the age of four when he signed up for PT boats in 1942.

PT-323 ENS Howard I. Green NY Daily News 4 Nov 1944

PT-323 ENS William Adelman Rauh Jewish Archives, Heinz History Center Pittsburgh

After the battle, on October 25th, Adelman wrote home to his wife. "For the past few days we have been quite busy with the Japs. Apparently they do not feel that our last move was in keeping with the Nipponese design of world conquest." 106

After sunrise, around 0630, when PT-323 was no longer in company with the other boats, she sighted a Japanese destroyer that appeared to be stopped and on fire. Radio communication with CTG 77.2 confirmed that the contact was not friendly. There was additional confirmation of this when the destroyer fired a couple

---

[106] Letter from LTJG Adelman to his wife – 25 Oct, 1944 William Ira Adelman Papers, 1943-1950,, Rauh Jewish Archives, Senator John Heinz History Center

of shots at 'Calamity Jane'. The boat closed in and made 3 separate approach runs at 8 knots. At the end of each run she released one Mark XIII torpedo at a range of about 1500 yards. The PT crew thought the last one might have scored (but it probably didn't) and she withdrew because heavier friendly units were approaching. The enemy ship had fired about 25 rounds at the PT, but most were very inaccurate and caused no damage.

This was the first time S1c (QM) James Archer from York was "Well initiated". 107 His battle station was in the chartroom or at the wheel of his PT-323.

"There was heavy shelling all around us," Archer said. "At times large shells landed within 1000 yards of our boat. One large piece of shrapnel hit the deck just a foot from me."108

He continued, "At dawn we sighted an enemy destroyer and fired three torpedoes at her. Shortly after there was an explosion and we believe it was our torpedo. The explosion tore the bow of the enemy ship off." 109

---

[107] The York Dispatch 19 Dec,1944 page20
[108] ibid
[109] ibid

Another crew member, slender RM3c Daniel Eddins Kirk, from North Carolina, had his overseas time temporarily cut short when he was injured in the kamikaze attack that destroyed PT-123. He ended the war wearing a Bronze Star, a Purple Heart, and a Presidential Unit Citation in addition to his service awards and victory medal.

PT-323 S1c (RM) Daniel Eddins Kirk 1943 Mars Hill College – ancestry.com

PT-323 MoMM3c Archie Jordan Freeman ancestry.com

After news of the battle reached his home town, Pittsburgh, The local Jewish paper, The Jewish Criterion, wrote about ENS Adelman, "We're glad and proud to have you there, Billy".110

PT 323, cut almost in half by a Kamikaze plane on December 10, 1944.

LTJG Adelman wrote the following letter to his wife on December 1st.

____

110Rauh Jewish Archives, Senator John Heinz History Center

(Reproduced with permission from William Ira Adelman Collection, Rauh Jewish Archives at the Heinz History Center).111

---

[111] Letter from LTJG Adelman to his wife – 1 Dec, 1944 William Ira Adelman Papers, 1943-1950,, Rauh Jewish Archives, Senator John Heinz History Center

Friday, December 1, 1944

Darling,

For the sake of a little variety, in this letter I'll try to tell you in detail just what I did today. It was a very uninteresting day, but here goes.

I got up at about 6:45 A.M., put on my khakis. By that time Herb had already tied up to the tender. We had our breakfast aboard. (Figs, 2 fried eggs sunny side up, bacon, toast and coffee). Since Herb "suggested" that I go to the brief again today, I changed into old clothes -- shorts and rubber boots. I took a few of our crew with me to the base -- we got a ride there from another PT boat. The boys were to draw our beer ration -- 5 cases! So, to the brief, where many interesting stories were told of last night's experiences plus intelligence reports etc. Then, back down the hill through the mud (I did come up it first) to one of the tents for a special squadron meeting. Then through more mud to the dock. It had started to rain at this point. As usual, I had no rain gear with me. I boarded another one of the boats, and we proceeded at an incredibly high speed to the tender. The time of arrival there was about 12:30. The beer had been brought back ahead of me, and when I came below, Herb was already distributing it. (It costs us .10¢ per can) Each man received about ten cans. Free cigarettes were also distributed -- about 14 packs per man. Since it was too late for chow aboard the tender, our cook made me two roast beef sandwiches -- bread, roast beef, and

2.

Ketchup, the slices of bread and roast beef being the same thickness. I also had a glass of lemonade. After that glorious repast, I had nothing to do, so I began studying some charts of our area. Jay Moody interrupted with a visit, told of his last night's patrol -- I showed him the newspaper clippings -- and he left. It had been raining constantly since morning, and I decided to hit the sack for a while. My attempt was frustrated by moving the boat from one side of the tender to the other. So, I went aboard, had a cup of coffee with Newcomb as we discussed the general PT situation here. Then, back to the boat and to another place where they put something back on with a crane. We dropped anchor at about five o'clock, and had evening chow. It consisted of hamburgers, potatoes (something like shoestring), highly seasoned cold cuts, more lemonade, and a large cookie. Immediately after, I began working on scraping the deck, using a blow torch and scraper. (Two of us work together). The rain had stopped for a while. It began again in sufficient force to make us stop work. So, here I am.

That's what happens, generally, day after day when you are not operating. It should be restful, but it isn't. If I am ever skipper, I'm going to have the boys take one whole day off. We'll drop anchor somewhere away from everybody, and sleep to our hearts content. (By the way, we go to sleep at 9:00 P.M. every night now, but it's so tempting to sleep when it rains all day.)

Let me tell you something of the nature of our duty. The following is naturally for private consumption only.

5

The work that we do requires a tremendous amount of
self control and discipline. I mean discipline against
fear. A man who is afraid on the boats is a
dangerous liability, not only to himself, but to others,
for fear is a contagion. It is the anticipation of what
may happen that is our principal enemy. It is most
emphatically a war of nerves. So far our nerves are
holding out pretty well. Everyone is afraid to a
greater or lesser degree, and in action they act on discipline
and reflex. A few show their fear and are unable
to control it. Any man who says he hasn't been almost
petrified by fear since he's been out here (if he's been
in action a number of times) isn't being honest with himself.
This fear is something that we all accept, and take for
granted as a normal reaction. We have learned to
live with it, and to a certain measure, control it. I was
really afraid once, quite recently. It's quite painless --
you are practically anesthetized by fear. (Everything
turned out all right -- see plane parts)

I'm writing you all this to give you a better under-
standing of the mental state of the men here. Everything
else, I mean everything other than fear, tends to
make us forget it or minimize it. As a result, very
few speak of it, and it is very much in the background.
And the Japs are scared silly of the boats!

As for me personally, -- by this time you probably
think that I'm frightened out of my wits! I suit my
emotions to the occasion. If it is something worthwhile,
my adrenalin will start flowing, too. This has been
the most rugged duty for PT's in this war, and I can
think of nothing that matches it. That phase is
past now, thank God, and our casualties were few.

4.

(Interruption)

I just returned from a consultation with our head engineer in our engine room. Things could be better here.

Its 4:10 P.m. and lights are going out.

Please take good care of yourself, darling. Get all the sleep you can. Give hands a big kiss for me.

I love you.

Bill

PT-323 survived the action in Surigao Straight only to be hit by a Japanese Kamikaze aircraft on December 10th, less than 2 months later.

PT-323 was proceeding down Surigao with PT-327 and 2 boats from MTBRON 36; PT-528 and PT-532. Four Japanese ZEKE fighters attacked them. Two of the Japanese attempted Kamikaze suicide attacks. One was shot down. The other hit PT-323. The aircraft struck the boat on the forward port torpedo and crushed the side of the wooden boat. The wing of the plane swept across the PT boat cockpit, toppling the radar mast. There was no fire and the wreckage of the boat remained afloat. Both the Jewish officers were killed.

There were 9 wounded among the PT-323 survivors taken aboard PT-327. Four others were pulled from the water. Most were taken to a nearby hospital ship, USS HOPE. Two weeks later twelve of the rescued crewmen were detached from MTBRON21 to be sent back to the USA for survivor's leave and possible reassignment. Survivor's leave was a grant of 30 days leave for crew members whose ship was sunk. They were given this extra time off while the Navy decided what to do with them. These are the names of the men from PT-323 that received the extra leave time:

F1c Warren Denison Mills from Michigan

GM3c Joseph John McDonald received 31 Aug 1944 without records

GM3c Raymond Edmond Chock from Minneapolis Minnesota

GM3c Lewis ('Sonny') Kessel from Galveston, Texas

F1c John Charles Rehak from Chicago, Illinois

MoMM2c Einrid Richard ('Bud') Neet from Oregon

MoMM3c Archie Jordan Freeman from Basset, Virginia

MoMM3c Herbert Harry Atzen from Delmar, Iowa

QM3c Robert Archer from North Carolina

RM3c Daniel Edins Kirk from Lewisville, North Carolina

SC1c Paul Arthur Baker from Sheridan, Indiana

SC3c Harry Ray Alexander from Willet, Pennsylvania

TM3c Richard Francis ('Dick') Lowe

LTJG Jack Mee also had a special post-war story. He had married before going overseas. When the war ended he returned to Toledo, Ohio, with his wife. But Jack was apparently not content with his life. He made arrangements to buy a former PT-boat, refurbished it as a civilian craft, and prepared to sail it to Cuba along with his friend, Charles Jackson, He was pursuing a former Toledo based exotic dancer named Patricia Schmidt. She used the stage name 'Satira'. Mee named his boat after her. Patricia was enamored, but soon found out that Mee already had a wife. When Mee tried to forcibly hold her on board his boat she managed to shoot and kill him (with his own gun). The scandalous story got wide coverage in all the papers in the US and Cuba.

PT-329 crewmen showing off the MTBRON21 emblem
ptboatforum.com

PT-329 Jack Mee's yacht Satira

23 Afterword

There were about 600 American sailors and officers in the 39 PT boats that participated in the Battle of Surigao Strait. One boat was lost and three sailors were killed during the battle. But the war was not over. In the text I have remembered 2 more boats that were lost in the two months following the battle.

Their crews are also remembered. I have included a number of photographs. Some are contemporary pictures of crew members, both before and during their service. A few others are post-war, including obituary pictures. Several came from surviving family members. The men shown are examples and the pictures are notable for the youth of those pictured in the earlier photos.

A total of 360 young men lost their lives while serving in PT-boats.

I tried to include actual quotes from the participants whenever I could. Some of those quotations are taken from newspaper accounts, Action Reports, and especially from the text of the book by David Sears, "Voices from Leyte".

I haven't always footnoted information that came from Muster Rolls, WWII Draft Cards, or similar sources.

The selection, or omission, of particular facts and items is by my choice, and I am the only one to blame for any errors of omission or commission.

These boat crews were part of what has become known as 'The Greatest Generation'.

I hope this book contributes to the reason they received that name.

Bibliography Notes:

I read a lot, especially on Kindle unlimited. But the most important sources were the action reports of the boats involved, the muster rolls of the MTBRONS, and items I found searching in newspaper archives, ancestry.com, fold3.com, and ptforum.com.

I own a copy of the Naval War college analysis of the battle that I also used about 20 years ago in my brief item at ptworld.com. Many photographs were taken from navsource.com, ancestry.com, and findagrave.com.

INDEX

Muller, ENS Robert Harold Jr., 171, 177
Myers, QM3c Joseph Nash, 151, 152, 156, 158, 187
Neet, MoMM2c Einrid Richard, 271
Nishimura, VADM Shoji, 54, 56
Norton, ENS H. F., 106
Oldendorf, RADM Jesse B., 227
Olton, LTJG Frank Hastings, 230, 237
Ormoc Bay, 65, 185, 237
Orrell, LT Robert Winfield, 165, 191, 192, 193
Owen, F2c Robert J., 106
Owen, LTJG Dwight H., 116, 118, 119, 122
Ozawa, VADM Jisaburo, 54
Panaon Island, 1, 69, 126, 130, 169, 198, 235
Parazinski, MoMM1c Robert John, 177
Parker, S1c Kenneth Eugene, 226, 227
Peterson, TM3c Arthur George, 205, 207, 208
Petrulavage, S1c George, 247, 248, 250
Ponson Island, 188
Pool, GM2c Clarence, 122
Poro Island, 188
Preston, LCDR Arthur Murray, 39, 68, 186, 188, 230, 231, 232
PT-127, 1, 23, 42, 75, 94, 97, 98, 100, 102, 103, 104, 105, 109, 110, 112, 114, 115, 164, 234
PT-128, 1, 97, 105, 106, 107, 108, 109, 113
PT-129, 1, 97, 103, 105, 106, 108, 112
PT-130, 1, 78, 79, 82, 85, 89, 90, 91, 93, 94, 95, 112
PT-131, 1, 78, 80, 94, 95, 96
PT-132, 59, 81, 164, 170, 171, 172, 173, 176, 178
PT-134, 1, 98, 164, 165, 167, 168, 169, 170, 174, 191

Into the Jaws of Death

Bibliography

Books (by Author)

Andruss, Frank J Sr.: PT Boats Behind the Scenes - Nimble Books Ann Arbor MI 2010

Andruss, Frank J Sr.: Building the PT Boats - Nimble Books Ann Arbor MI 2010

Andruss, Frank J Sr.: Pieces of History Artifacts of the PT Boat Navy - Nimble books Ann Arbor MI 2020

Angel, Byron: PT Boats Attack - kindle unlimited

Baron, Scott: The Hooligan Navy - kindle unlimited

Beck, James: Southwest Pacific Motor Torpedo Boats - kindle unlimited – (A Terrible book -near fiction!)

Breuer, William: - Devil Boats Presidio Press CA 1987

Brock, Lilly Robbins Wooden Boats and Iron Men - kindle unlimited

Bulkeley, Robert J.: At Close Quarters USNI Press 2003

Chun, Victor: American Pt Boats in World War II Vol 1 & Vol 2

Desloge, Rick: Hell on Keels MTBRON 12 history - kindle unlimited

Doyle. David: Elco 80 foot PT Boat Squadron/Signal publications, Texas 2009

Doyle, David: PT Boats: The US Navy's Fast Attack Patrol Torpedo Bots in World War II - kindle unlimited

Engelmann, Michael: Epic Voyage: The Greatest PT Boat Story Never Told - kindle unlimited

Norman Friedman, U S Small Combatants including PT Boats, Subchasers, and the Brown-Water Navy: An illustrated design history USNI Press

Hart, Thomas: PT Squadron 16: World War II Memories - kindle unlimited

Holmes, W.J. Double-edged Secrets = US Naval Institute Press, Annapolis, MD. 1979

Lewin, Ronald: The Other Ultra Hutchinson, London 1982

Morison, S.E.: History of United States Naval Operations in WWII Vol XII Leyte Little, Brown and Co. Boston 1975

Prescott, Kenneth W: A PT Skipper in the South Pacific - kindle unlimited

Rottman Gordon L.: US Patrol Torpedo Boats World War II - Osprey 2008

Sears, David: The Last Epic Naval Battle: Voices From Leyte Gulf - Greenwood publishing group 2005

Skimarkas, F. J.: Devil Boats -Stackpole 2023

Into the Jaws of Death

Tully Anthon P.: The Battle of Surigao Strait – Univ. of Indiana Press Apr 2003

White, W.L.: They Were Expendable Harcourt & Brace NY 1942

Young American Patriots - Youth of Ohio in World War II National Publishing Co Richmond VA 1947

US Government publications:

Office of Naval History - An Administrative History of PT's in World War II – 1946

Navy Dept., Know Your PT Boat Bureau of Ships Technical Pub 9 NAVSHIPS 250-222-1 15 Jul 1945

US Navy Registers especially Jul 1944 at ancestry.com, Univ. of Oregon microfilmed copy

Officer Yearbooks: USNA Lucky Bag, OCS Columbia U NY Sideboy, OCS Cornell U Archway, OCS Fort Schuyler NY Gangway, OCS Notre Dame Capstan

USNWC: The Battle for Leyte Gulf - Vol V Battle of Surigao St Navpers 92628 1958

USSBS Naval analysis division: Campaigns of the Pacific War = GPO Washington 1946

USSBS: Interrogation of Japanese Officers #75 ADM Soemu Toyoda

Navy Dept.: Muster rolls from MTB squadrons 7, 12 21 33 and 36

Navy Dept.: Action Reports - from CTG70.1 (Commander, MTBs Seventh Fleet) and others

Seaman, Donald: "Intelligence in the Fleet" Naval Engineers Journal 1963. pp 61-64

Brown, R. William: "They called her 'Carole Baby'" Naval History magazine Oct 2001 p23-25

Internet sources:

ancestry.com

findagrave.com

fold3.com

history.net: David Sears = Wooden Boats At War: Surigao Strait -

pt127.org

ptboatforum.com -

ptsinc.com

ptworld.com: Aryeh Wetherhorn - PTs at Surigao -

National WWII Museum new Orleans website: Joshua Schick - A Horticulturist Goes to War = 21 Apr. 2020

navsource.org: especially PT 493 entry - "Surigao Strait"

rauhjewisharchives.org/entry/Adelman-family/

Into the Jaws of Death

Terryfoundation.org- Edward T Cotham Jr = A PT Captain in the Pacific, Howard L Terry's World War II Service

The Mosquito Fleet Exhibit WWII PT BOATS -Facebook group

Newspaper items:

Newspaperrchives.com

Chronicling America @ Library of Congress

Martin Sheridan Boston Globe (war correspondent} reports in various papers

Stanton Delaplane (war correspondent} reports in various papers

SGT Henry McLemore (army war correspondent) reports in various papers

Jack Turcott - NY Daily News 4 Nov 44 - Green, D'Amico Obituary columns in various papers

Other wartime press releases about local residents in the military in various papers

Toledo Gazette - especially articles by Lou Hebert about LTJG Jack Mee and Satira - 2010 and 2016